T0031522

What's the *Big Deal* ABOUT ADDICTIONS?

ANSWERS and HELP for TEENS

JAMES J. CRIST, PH.D., C.S.A.C.

free spirit
PUBLISHING®

Text copyright © 2021 by James J. Crist

All rights reserved under International and Pan-American Copyright Conventions. Unless otherwise noted, no part of this book may be reproduced, stored in a retrieval system, or transmitted in any form or by any means, electronic, mechanical, photocopying, recording, or otherwise, without express written permission of the publisher, except for brief quotations or critical reviews. For more information, go to freespirit.com/permissions.

Free Spirit, Free Spirit Publishing, and associated logos are trademarks and/or registered trademarks of Free Spirit Publishing Inc. A complete listing of our logos and trademarks is available at freespirit.com.

Library of Congress Cataloging-in-Publication Data
Names: Crist, James J., author.
Title: What's the big deal about addictions? : answers and help for teens / James J. Crist, Ph.D., C.S.A.C.
Description: Minneapolis : Free Spirit Publishing Inc., 2021. | Includes bibliographical references. | Audience: Ages 13+
Identifiers: LCCN 2020036069 (print) | LCCN 2020036070 (ebook) | ISBN 9781631985300 (paperback) | ISBN 9781631985317 (pdf) | ISBN 9781631985324 (epub)
Subjects: LCSH: Teenagers—Substance use—Juvenile literature. | Teenagers—Drug use—Juvenile literature. | Teenagers—Alcohol use—Juvenile literature. | Compulsive behavior—Juvenile literature.
Classification: LCC HV4999.Y68 C75 2021 (print) | LCC HV4999.Y68 (ebook) | DDC 613.80835—dc23
LC record available at https://lccn.loc.gov/2020036069
LC ebook record available at https://lccn.loc.gov/2020036070

Free Spirit Publishing does not have control over or assume responsibility for author or third-party websites and their content. At the time of this book's publication, all facts and figures cited within are the most current available. All telephone numbers, addresses, and website URLs are accurate and active; all publications, organizations, websites, and other resources exist as described in this book; and all have been verified as of July 2020. If you find an error or believe that a resource listed here is not as described, please contact Free Spirit Publishing. Parents, teachers, and other adults: We strongly urge you to monitor children's use of the internet.

Note to readers: This book contains information and advice about addictions. The concepts, ideas, and suggestions contained here should not replace professional medical and psychiatric treatment.

Reading Level Grade 7; Interest Level Ages 13 & up;
Fountas & Pinnell Guided Reading Level Z

Edited by Cassie Sitzman
Cover and interior design by Emily Dyer

10 9 8 7 6 5 4 3 2 1
Printed in the United States of America
V20301220

Free Spirit Publishing Inc.
6325 Sandburg Road, Suite 100
Minneapolis, MN 55427-3674
(612) 338-2068
help4kids@freespirit.com
freespirit.com

FSC
www.fsc.org
MIX
Paper from
responsible sources
FSC® C005010

Free Spirit offers competitive pricing.
Contact edsales@freespirit.com for pricing information on multiple quantity purchases.

Dedication

I'd like to dedicate this book to all the teens I've worked with who have struggled with addictions of various sorts. I admire their courage and persistence in working toward beating their addictions and living happier, healthier lives.

• • • • •

Acknowledgments

I want to thank psychiatrist Dr. Amelia Withington, my college friend and colleague, for her review of the manuscript as well as her helpful additions from a medical perspective. I would also like to thank my graduate school classmate Sheila Phillips, M.A., and my first supervisor when working at Alexandria Substance Abuse Services, Phil Keller, M.A., C.A.C., Esq., for triggering my interest in, and teaching me about, alcohol and drug abuse treatment and convincing me to pursue this further. I want to thank Ron Hughes and Larry Fabian for their support in working with the Metropolitan Alcohol Center when I started my practice after finishing my internship. I'd like to thank school social worker Vicky Castro, M.S.W., who encouraged me to write this book a few years ago, as it is a much-needed resource for today's young people. Finally, I would like to thank my editor, Cassie Sitzman, for her guidance and help in reviewing the manuscript and for making so many excellent suggestions.

Contents

Introduction

Anthony looks forward to hanging out with his lacrosse team buddies after games. Sometimes his teammates bring a six-pack of beer or some Jack Daniels to celebrate their wins. While laughing and joking with his friends seems harmless, Anthony can't help but think about what their coach told the team at the beginning of the season: they can get kicked off the team permanently if they drink or use drugs.

Adrian spends a lot of time gaming. Most of their weekends are spent in front of a screen. Adrian's parents complain about how much time Adrian spends online, but Adrian says it's okay because that's where their friends are.

Julian enjoys smoking weed with his friends. He does it mostly on the weekends, and since he doesn't do it every weekend, he figures he doesn't have a problem. Lately, though, he has started using more during the week because it helps him relax and get to sleep.

Keiko started using by experimenting with prescription drugs she found in her parents' medicine cabinet. Vicodin seemed interesting, and she tried it with her friends. They found that they liked the high they got from it, especially when they took more pills than recommended on the bottle. Keiko and her friends liked the feeling so much that they started raiding the medicine cabinets of their other friends and family members.

You may know teens like Anthony, Adrian, Julian, and Keiko. Maybe you can relate to their stories. Seems like their behavior is pretty harmless, right? What's so bad about having alcohol at a party, staying up late gaming, smoking a joint with friends, or sneaking a few prescription pills from your parents' medicine cabinet? While some teens might never get caught and it seems like they're not having problems as a result, many find their lives turned upside down by activities like these. Fighting with parents or friends, missing class because you're too tired to get up, losing privileges, earning lower grades, and even being expelled from school or getting arrested are just a few of the problems that can happen when alcohol, drugs, or other activities become addictive.

Why I Wrote This Book

I thought about writing this book for a long time before I actually sat down to write it. I started out as a substance abuse counselor for a city agency, where I worked with adults addicted to heroin, alcohol, cocaine, and PCP. Throughout my career, I've continued to work with people who have addictions, and many of my current clients are teens. What I've found is that while some teens are able to use drugs or alcohol on occasion, others can't control their use, even after their parents find out, they get kicked out of school, or they end up on probation or in juvenile detention. I've also learned that just telling people to stop, or yelling at them about consequences (which is what many adults do), doesn't really help. Listening respectfully, appreciating the reasons why people use drugs and alcohol, and having a conversation about the pros and cons is much more helpful.

Since finding out about the many similarities between substance addictions (drugs and alcohol) and other addictions (such as tech, gaming, social media, self-injury, gambling, and so on), I have been able to use the same strategies that help people addicted to drugs and alcohol to help people who have problems with a variety of activities. And now I'm sharing this knowledge with you.

How This Book Can Help

This book will give you reliable and factual information about alcohol, drugs, and other addictions, without the lecturing you might hear elsewhere. You'll also learn how many teens actually use drugs and alcohol. There's a lot of misinformation out there, and you need to know about the risks involved so you can make informed decisions about activities that affect your relationships, health, and wellness.

You'll learn the difference between casual use and addictive use and how to figure out if you (or a family member or a friend) really have a problem. You'll find out about the possible consequences of risky behavior, ways to help yourself feel good without drugs and alcohol, and things you can do to overcome your addictions. Straightforward information about the various treatment options is provided, as well as proven tips to keep you from slipping back into old habits and help you avoid relapse.

Maybe you've never had a problem with addictive substances or behaviors. This book can help you too. In it you'll find answers to your questions about alcohol, drugs, and other activities as well as tips to help you avoid developing an addiction in the future.

Of course, reading this book doesn't replace getting professional help if you have a chemical or behavioral addiction. Talk to your parents or guardians, or another trusted adult such as a doctor, school counselor, teacher, or coach, if you think you need help. If you are already getting help for an addiction, talking with your doctor or therapist about the information you learn in this book might help you get better faster.

How to Use This Book

You can read this book cover-to-cover or skip around to find the parts most relevant to you.

Chapter 1 gives you an overview of drug and alcohol addictions in teens, including how common they are and how to tell the difference between casual use and addictive use. You'll learn what a substance use disorder is and how to tell if you have it. Examples of benefits of using drugs and alcohol, as well as negative consequences of using them, are provided.

Chapter 2 explains more about alcohol use. You'll learn what a blood alcohol concentration is and how the amount you drink affects your behavior and your health. Information on drinking alcohol responsibly, should you choose to drink, is provided.

Chapter 3 reviews similar information regarding drug use. Various drugs people abuse are reviewed, as well as some of the risks involved with each. Information about how drug use can lead to legal consequences is included.

Chapter 4 covers addiction to tech (electronics), such as gaming, phone use, and social media, and how to tell if you might have a problem. Suggestions on how to monitor your use and avoid a tech addiction are provided, along with a brief overview of cyberbullying and how to handle it.

Chapter 5 focuses on activity addictions, such as addiction to food, sex, self-injury, shopping, and gambling. You'll learn how to tell if these are just bad habits or if they're addictions that cause problems for you.

Chapter 6 shares ways to get help with addictive behaviors, including figuring out if you are ready to quit. You'll learn about the stages of recovery, symptoms of withdrawal, the different types of treatment for addictions, how support groups can help, and how the presence of other disorders (such as ADHD or depression) can make treatment more challenging.

Chapter 7 gives you strategies that can help you keep from slipping back into addictions and shares ways to help you feel good without using drugs, alcohol, or other addictive activities. These include learning to identify your triggers and warning signs for relapse, learning to manage your emotions, and finding healthier substitutes for addictive behaviors. Information regarding drug testing and how to cope if you do relapse is provided.

Finally, the **glossary** includes a variety of terms used in this book, and the **resources** point you toward places you can go for help and more information.

As you read, try to keep an open mind. You're probably used to adults telling you that should never use alcohol or drugs, that you have a problem, or that you should give up your gaming or social media habit completely. No one likes being nagged about their behavior and it would be easy to just tune these people out and assume that they're overreacting. But what if they're not? Wouldn't it be a good idea to find out for yourself? Even if you're not sure about yourself, you may recognize some of your family members or friends in this book. By sharing what you learn with them, you might be able to help them too. Either way, you'll have more information that you can use to make important decisions about yourself and your life.

CHAPTER 1

What's the Big Deal About Addictions?

Bethany likes using marijuana. It helps her relax and makes many of her activities more fun, even just watching TV or playing video games. At first, she made money for weed by selling it to kids at school. But after getting caught and being suspended, she figured it was time to stop. After a few weeks, though, she started craving it and thought it wouldn't hurt to use every once in a while. She thought she could limit her use, but now she has started smoking more often, even though she knows her grandparents are drug testing her.

Nico likes using his e-cigarette in the school bathroom with his friends. It's fun trying to sneak around school officials, and it gives him a boost for the day. Besides, he's been able to meet a whole new group of friends just by vaping. Nico also has a part-time job, so he uses some of that money to buy the pods from an older coworker and sell them to his friends.

Are these teens just having fun? Are their behaviors harmless, or are they starting to cause trouble? How much is too much? Where do you draw the line?

You've probably heard people tell you that *any* drug or alcohol use as a teenager is bad, that it can cause lifelong problems. But is this true? In this chapter, you'll learn how to tell the difference between casual use and addictive use of substances, how many teens actually use drugs and alcohol, and some of the effects drug and alcohol use can have, both negative and positive. You'll learn more about other addictions, such as gaming, porn, and social media, and how to spot problems with them in chapters 4 and 5.

A NOTE ON TERMS

Abuse and *addiction* are similar terms. Both cause problems in your life. But generally, abuse is less severe and may only cause temporary consequences physically, socially, and psychologically. Addiction is more serious. People with an addiction use more often, in greater amounts, and have lasting physical consequences, including changes to their brains. Most people with addiction experience withdrawal symptoms, such as irritability, sleep disturbance, or even physical pain.

Casual Use or Addictive Use?

"I don't do it all the time, so I can't be addicted."

• • • •

"Smoking weed is the only way I can fall asleep. I can still get up in the morning."

For many teens, occasional use of a substance may never cause a problem. They don't lose sleep, get in trouble, get lower grades, or feel worse after using. It may not be a wise choice to use, since using is illegal for teens, but they know when to stop. You must be 21 to purchase cigarettes, e-cigarettes, and alcohol in the United States. In states where marijuana is legal, you also have to be at least 21 to purchase it for recreational use and 18 for medical use.* However, this doesn't stop some teens from using. Here's an example:

Maria drinks alcohol with her friends on the weekends. Not every weekend, just when she hangs out with friends. Her parents don't know about her use, and she only has a couple beers or malt beverages at a time, just enough to catch a buzz. She doesn't get drunk and she has never done anything dangerous while drinking, such as driving, and hasn't done anything she later regretted.

Maria's use doesn't seem to be causing problems, at least not yet. She doesn't think her use is a big deal. But for other people, once they start using, they want to do it more and more often, and in greater and greater amounts. These are the people who are most likely to get addicted. Once this happens, continuing to use drugs or alcohol can cause serious problems. It can affect your physical health, your mental health, your grades, your relationships, and your work. It can also get you in trouble with the law.

Even Occasional Use Can Lead to Addiction

"I was always really anxious as a kid. I'd worry about everything. Once I started drinking, it seemed like my fears disappeared and I could talk to people at a party or even go up to a girl I liked. But while my friends were able to stop after a while, I always wanted more. Two beers turned into 10 beers. It wasn't until I started driving home drunk after parties that I realized I had a problem."

• • • •

---

* If you don't live in the United States, you'll need to see what age restrictions are in your area.

"I always felt like something was missing in my life—that I couldn't feel happy like some of my friends. My boyfriend tried to help by introducing me to coke. At first, I said no—I didn't see myself as a drug user. But after he convinced me, I tried snorting my first line of coke at a party. It was amazing! The bad feelings disappeared, and I felt on top of the world! At first, I only did it once in a while, but after a few months, I found myself using daily. I couldn't handle the comedown when it wore off. I spent most of my summer earnings on drugs and had nothing to show for it."

Addiction is a compulsive need for a habit-forming substance or activity. This need can be physical, psychological, or both. Not everyone who uses alcohol or drugs goes on to become addicted. Most adults, for example, can have a few drinks and know when to stop, and their use doesn't cause problems for them in their lives. However, most people who smoke cigarettes do get addicted. It is one of the hardest habits to break.

The first few times someone uses alcohol or drugs, it's generally a choice. Maybe someone at a party offered you a cigarette, a blunt, a pill, or a beer and you decided to give it a try. No one is forcing you to do it, and you can decide to stop whenever you want. But when you use a substance repeatedly, your brain changes and you may want to use more often and in greater amounts.

Brain chemistry plays a large part in addictions. Most people seek out addictive activities for three basic reasons: wanting to relax or reduce anxiety, looking for excitement and stimulation, and wanting to alter their perceptions to have an interesting experience. (For ways feel good without resorting to drugs and alcohol, see the sidebar on page 17. Chapter 7 also shares ideas to help you stay away from drugs, alcohol, and other addictive activities.) People can also be motivated by more than

How to Interpret Percentages

If a statistic says that 20 percent of teens use alcohol, this means that out of every 100 teens, 20 of them use alcohol and 80 do not. A statistic of 50 percent means half of all teens use alcohol.

one reason at a time. Most addictions (including activity addictions) increase the production of the brain chemical dopamine. Increasing dopamine makes activities more enjoyable and can make people want to do more of the ones they like, even to excess. However, the human body eventually gets used to whatever new stimulation it's provided, making the activity less rewarding. As a result, a person needs to have more and more of the substance (or to spend more and more time on the activity) to feel good. This is called increasing tolerance, which is a warning sign of addiction.

Since addiction often runs in families, some of a person's potential for addiction is genetic, meaning that if you have family members with addiction problems, the chances are greater that you'll have problems too.

Substance Use Disorder

Mental health counselors call addiction to substances, including alcohol and drugs, substance use disorders. Essentially, substance use becomes a disorder when a person keeps using drugs or alcohol even after it starts to cause them problems. Symptoms fall into one of four categories:

1. Loss of control over your use

2. Problems getting along with others as a result of your use

3. Using when it is risky or dangerous to do so (for example, driving a car or bike or performing other activities, such as skateboarding, after using alcohol or drugs)

4. Physical changes in your body (needing more to get the same effect—called tolerance) or symptoms of withdrawal (such as being grouchy, having trouble sleeping, or being more anxious) when you stop using the substance

Frequency of Teen Use of Alcohol and Other Drugs

Just how many teens are using alcohol and drugs? You might think that everybody uses alcohol or drugs, especially if most of your friends use, but this is not true. Here are some recent nationwide statistics from the US Centers for Disease Control and Prevention (CDC) and the National Institute on Drug Abuse (NIDA), based on surveys of teenage students.

Alcohol

- 58.5% of 12th graders had had at least one drink of alcohol during their life
- 29.2% of students had had at least one drink of alcohol in the last 30 days

Nicotine

- 24.1% of students had ever tried smoking cigarettes
- 6% of students had smoked cigarettes at least once during the last 30 days
- 50.1% of students had ever used an electronic vapor product (including e-cigarettes, vaping pipes or pens, e-hookahs, and hookah pens)
- 32.7% of students had used an electronic vapor product at least once during the last 30 days

Marijuana

- 36.8% of students had used marijuana (grass, pot, or weed) one or more times during their life
- 21.7% of students had used marijuana one or more times during the last 30 days
- 14% of 12th graders had vaped marijuana in the past month

Other drugs

- 7.3% of students had ever used synthetic marijuana (also called K2, Spice, Fake Weed, King Kong, Yucatan Fire, Skunk, or Moon Rocks)
- 3.9% of students had ever used any form of cocaine (powder, crack, or freebase)
- 6.2% of students had ever sniffed glue, breathed the contents of aerosol spray cans, or inhaled any paints or sprays
- 1.8% of students had ever used heroin
- 2.1% of students had ever used methamphetamines (also called Speed, Crystal, Crank, or Ice)
- 4% of students had ever used ecstasy (MDMA, also called Molly)
- 6.6% of students had ever used hallucinogenic drugs (LSD, acid, PCP, mescaline, or mushrooms)
- 14.3% of students had ever taken prescription pain medicine (including drugs such as codeine, Vicodin, OxyContin, hydrocodone, and Percocet) without a doctor's prescription or differently than how a doctor told them to use it
- 7.7% of 12th graders had misused Adderall and 2% had abused the stimulant Ritalin

So, not every teen uses drugs or alcohol. But if are you around people who use frequently, it sure can seem that way! One reason for this is that people who drink alcohol or use drugs (even just smoking cigarettes) tend to hang together, and people who don't use tend to hang together. That makes it harder to figure out how many other teens are actually using.

IS ADDICTION A DISEASE?

In a sense, yes. Addiction changes how the brain works and affects your ability to function at your best. It also has the potential to kill you if you use too much or use in situations that are dangerous, such as driving when under the influence. The changes to your brain and your ability to function can be permanent. For example, you can suffer a stroke if you abuse cocaine, which damages the brain.

Read through the following symptoms of a substance use disorder. While not all of these symptoms occur with all substances, this list will give you an idea of what signs to look for in figuring out whether your use (or someone else's) is a problem.

- Using larger amounts, or over a longer time, than you planned. Maybe you intended to have two beers, but once you started, you drank a lot more. It's hard to stop once you start.

- Wanting to stop or being unsuccessful in using less or stopping your use. You might have good intentions or make promises to yourself or others to control your use, but you can't keep those promises.

- Spending a lot of time getting, using, or recovering from a substance. For example, blowing off your homework or chores to find ways to get and use drugs, or using so much that you can't get up for school or work the next day.

- Having strong cravings to keep using. You might want to stop, but cravings make you want to use anyway. This is one of the changes in your brain that happens with repeated use of a drug or alcohol.

- Failing to meet your responsibilities (at school, home, or work) as a result of your use. Skipping school or calling in sick to work because you are hungover are examples of this. So is being unable to study for a test because you were high or drunk.

- Continuing to use drugs or alcohol while knowing that you have problems that are caused or made worse by your use. For example, fighting with your parents over your use or seeing your grades drop doesn't make you want to stop.

- Repeated use in situations that are dangerous, such as driving after drinking or using drugs. (This is also illegal.)

- Continuing to use while knowing you have physical or psychological problems that are caused or made worse by your use. Even though you don't get enough sleep or get more depressed after you use a drug, you still keep using.

- Increased tolerance (needing more to get the same effect). This happens because your body gets better at breaking down alcohol or drugs. Maybe two beers were enough to get you buzzed when you first started drinking, but now it takes four or more to get the same effect.

- Withdrawal (having symptoms such as irritability, depression, or sleep disturbance) when you suddenly stop using. For example, although some people believe

ADDICTION STARTS EARLY

The earlier in your life you start using drugs or alcohol, the greater your chances are of having problems later.* Why is this? The teen brain is growing and developing rapidly, and this growth doesn't start to slow down until about age 25. If your brain develops expecting to get a drug on a regular basis, the need for it gets "hardwired" into your brain. This makes it harder to stop later, since you may not feel normal without the drug. Life may seem dull (even the things you used to think were fun) if you aren't using drugs or alcohol.

For example, NIDA reports that about 30 percent of people who use marijuana will become addicted to it. That's about three out of every 10 people. But people who start using marijuana before age 18 are four to seven times more likely to develop a marijuana use disorder compared to those who used only as an adult.

---

* If you want to read more about this, the National Institute on Drug Abuse (NIDA) publishes information about the science behind addiction on their website: drugabuse.gov/publications/drugs-brains-behavior-science-addiction.

that marijuana is not addictive, many have trouble sleeping when they stop using it, especially if they used it to help them sleep. Getting irritable or angry is another withdrawal symptom of regular marijuana use.

Risk Factors for Addiction

One thing you should think about in deciding whether to use drugs or alcohol is how likely it is that you will develop a problem. While you can't know for sure if you are at greater risk for developing an addiction, there are certain things that increase your risk. These include:

- having a family member who is abusing or has abused drugs or alcohol
- having mental health problems such as anxiety or depression
- hanging with friends who use drugs or alcohol
- doing poorly in school
- having family conflict
- having been physically or sexually abused

The type of drug you use and how you use it also affects your risk. Injecting (shooting up) or smoking a drug such as heroin or cocaine is more addictive than sniffing it. These ways of using allow the drug to travel to the brain faster, which increases the risk for addiction. Nicotine products (cigarettes, e-cigarettes, or vaping) are especially addictive because nicotine doesn't stay in your system that long and using multiple times a day increases your risk.

While vaping marijuana can be less irritating on your throat than smoking a joint or blunt, it also delivers higher doses of THC (tetrahydrocannabinol, the active compound in marijuana that gets you high). This increases your exposure and makes the effects of the THC more intense, such as slowing your reaction times, impairing your memory, and even causing you to hallucinate.

Simply being a teenager is a risk factor as well, because the younger you start using drugs or alcohol, the more likely you are to become addicted. Also, the more often you use, and the greater the amount you use, the greater your chances are of becoming addicted. The safest approach is to wait until you are older, if you choose to use alcohol or drugs at all.

IS MARIJUANA A GATEWAY DRUG?

In a sense, yes. Most people who use marijuana do not go on to use other drugs. But almost all users of other drugs start with marijuana. That's why the safest approach is not to use at all, especially if you have other family members with addiction problems.

Benefits of Using Drugs and Alcohol

Clearly, use of alcohol or drugs has some benefits—otherwise, why use at all? People use drugs or alcohol for many reasons, including to:

- relax
- forget about problems
- lower anxiety
- sleep better
- be more social
- have more fun or celebrate
- feel less depressed
- feel less angry
- have new experiences
- boost creativity
- be accepted by the crowd
- relieve boredom

Some people self-medicate with alcohol or drugs. This means that they are treating a psychological or physical problem, such as depression, anxiety, or chronic pain, by using. However, the effects don't last. While drugs and alcohol might help at first, they often lead to problems the longer a person uses. This is also true of tech addictions and other activity addictions. It starts out helping, but then becomes part of the problem.

Also, if a person is taking medication to help with a psychological or physical problem, drug or alcohol use can keep the medicine from working. And some drugs are dangerous when combined with psychiatric medications. For example, if you take Ritalin or Adderall for ADHD and drink a lot of alcohol with it, your risk for having a seizure, stroke, or heart attack increases. Taking the antidepressant Wellbutrin increases your risk for a seizure if you drink heavily. These are just two examples. If you are taking any kind of medication, be honest with your doctor about any other drugs you are using, including alcohol and nicotine.

Consequences of Using Drugs and Alcohol

Let's face it—you probably aren't thinking about years down the road. Just figuring out how you'll get that research paper done and turned in by tomorrow may seem overwhelming! However, you may want to give the future some thought, since the choices you make now can affect how well you will function years from now.

For example, long-term use of alcohol and other drugs can result in memory problems, lower grades, difficulty getting and keeping jobs, and greater health problems. Depression is often made worse by using drugs or alcohol. Some people who use become paranoid, thinking others are out to get them. Damage can occur to the heart, liver, and kidneys that causes problems later in life, or even leads to death. Cirrhosis of the liver occurs when the liver stops working after years of alcohol use. Again, you might not be thinking of what will happen years from now, but the damage builds up over time.

Drug and alcohol use can also cause legal problems. If you are arrested for driving while drunk or under the influence of alcohol or other substances, you can lose your driver's license and may have to pay a large fine. Hiring an attorney likely costs thousands of dollars. If you don't have money for an attorney, you can ask for a court-appointed one. But these lawyers often have a lot of cases and may not be able to spend much time on yours. A

Ways to Feel Good without Drugs and Alcohol ⚡ TIP!

While some people use drugs, alcohol, and other activities like gaming as a way to deal with uncomfortable emotions and avoid boredom, there are lots of ways you can help yourself feel good without these activities. Alex Packer, the author of the book *Wise Highs: How to Thrill, Chill, and Get Away from It All Without Alcohol or Other Drugs*, surveyed 2,000 kids and teens ages 11 to 18 about ways they relieve stress and other emotions without drugs and alcohol. Coping strategies shared include:

- breathing deeply
- watching TV
- exercising
- playing a sport
- talking with friends and family
- sleeping
- singing
- playing music
- getting a hug
- playing board games
- reading
- writing in a journal or diary
- cooking
- going for a drive
- telling jokes
- making a video
- painting
- meditating
- getting outdoors
- listening to soothing sounds

Trying one of these ideas when you're stressed, upset, or bored is a healthier option. Chapters 6 and 7 share even more ways to help you keep busy and relieve stress without drugs and alcohol.

court-appointed attorney might even meet you for the first time on your court date.

You can lose your job if you test positive for drugs. Many companies require you to pass a drug test before being hired too. Bringing drugs can cause you to lose privileges at school, such as participating in sports or after-school clubs, attending dances or other school events, or leaving campus for lunch. It can get you expelled. That won't look good on a college application! If you are convicted of a felony (such as drunk driving or selling drugs), it can stay on your record for your entire life and can disqualify you for student loans and for many jobs, including enlisting in military service or getting a security clearance.

Finally, drug use changes your brain and how it operates, making it harder for you to enjoy the everyday activities that make life worth living. Normal activities can seem boring compared to the excitement you feel when you're drunk or high. This is what makes substances so hard for many people to quit. And the younger you start using, the more likely you are to change your brain permanently because your brain isn't fully developed.

Can Teens Use Drugs and Alcohol Responsibly?

This is a tricky question. Some people don't think it is ever okay for teens to use drugs or alcohol. And since drugs and alcohol are illegal to possess as a teen, you are breaking the law by using, even if you don't think you will get caught. Even keeping drugs for a friend can get you in big trouble. And drug and alcohol use as a teen may hurt your body and brain more severely than if you were using as an adult. Using can also cause a great deal of family conflict. Your parents or guardians may start watching your every move, go through your belongings, check your phone, and make life miserable for you because they are scared that something bad will happen to you.

Many substance abuse counselors follow a harm-reduction model in helping people who use drugs or alcohol. While the safest approach is not to use at all, if you choose to use, the less you use, the safer you'll be. For example, drinking a couple beers with friends at a party where you aren't driving home is less risky than playing beer pong and having 10 or more beers. And some drugs are much riskier than others. People overdose and die using drugs such as cocaine, heroin, crystal meth, and ecstasy. Alcohol can kill you if you drink too much. While people don't overdose on marijuana, they can become paranoid and hallucinate. Cigarettes may not cause significant problems when you first use, but they increase your risk for many health problems such as heart attacks and lung cancer when you're older. Limiting your use makes it less likely that it will cause problems.

Addictions can cause serious problems for teens. While no one ever plans on getting addicted to substances, tech, or other activities, an addiction can sneak up on you and before you know it, you're in trouble. The more you understand the risks involved with addictive behavior, the better able you will be to make smart choices. The next several chapters share information about specific substance use problems as well as information about electronics and other activity addictions.

CHAPTER 2

Alcohol Use— Just the Facts

"I've never felt good about myself. I hate exercising and have always struggled with my weight. I found that at parties, I have a much better time if I'm drinking. A few hard lemonades and maybe some shots loosen me up and guys seem to notice me more."

• • • •

"I have been drinking and smoking weed since I was 15. It was fun with friends, even though I drank way more than they did. I spent most of the money I earned working as a lifeguard on drugs and alcohol. After I came home drunk again, my parents threatened to kick me out of the house or send me to rehab if I didn't stop. I'm not sure what it was, but thinking about all my parents have done for me and how scared they were every time I left the house, I decided it was time to quit. The first couple weeks were rough, but then it got better. Not only did I lose weight, but I actually felt happy for the first time in months."

Alcohol use is fairly common among teenagers. As you learned in chapter 1, more than half of teens (60.4 percent) have had at least one drink of alcohol in their life. But far fewer drink on a regular basis. In this chapter, you'll learn more about alcohol and its effects, as well as the risks you need to know about if you drink or spend time around others who drink.

Types of Alcohol

Alcohol (ethanol or ethyl alcohol) is the active ingredient in beer, wine, liquor, and canned cocktails. Each contains a different percentage of alcohol. This means that the amount of liquid in your glass, can, or bottle doesn't always tell you how much alcohol is in your drink. In the United States, the standard drink size contains about 14 grams of pure alcohol. This is the amount of alcohol found in:

- 12 ounces of beer (about 5% alcohol)
- 8 ounces of malt liquor—beer with a high alcohol content (about 7% alcohol)
- 5 ounces of wine (about 12% alcohol)
- 1.5 ounces (one shot) of liquor, such as gin, rum, vodka, tequila, or whiskey (generally about 40–50% alcohol)

Wine coolers have about 5 percent alcohol in them, as well as more sugar than regular wine. Canned cocktails, including hard ciders and lemonades, can contain anywhere from 3 to 9 percent alcohol and have more sugar than beer, wine, or liquor. While sweeter drinks can slow the effects of alcohol, the sugar also makes it harder to know just how much you are drinking.

In the United States, you will see liquor bottles with the amount of alcohol described as the "proof." For example, 100 proof alcohol means that alcohol makes up 50 percent of the contents of the bottle. Most whiskeys and vodkas are about 100 proof.

Everclear vodka is about 190 proof, making it much stronger and more dangerous since it can raise your blood alcohol level quickly.

Alcohol is a depressive drug. This means that it depresses, or slows, your breathing and heart rate, which gives it a calming effect on many people. Since it also slows the control centers of the brain, alcohol can have a stimulating effect too (make you feel "buzzed") because it lowers your inhibitions. In greater amounts, it slows you down and impairs your ability to function, such as when you drink enough to get drunk.

Blood Alcohol Concentration

Your blood alcohol concentration, or BAC (also known as your blood alcohol level), is the amount of alcohol present in your bloodstream. Most people can process about one drink per hour, though this varies depending on your weight, your sex,[*] how recently you've eaten, how fast you drink, and what other drugs you might have used before or after drinking. Your liver is the organ that processes most of the alcohol you consume, and when you drink more than one drink an hour, the alcohol backs up in your bloodstream as it waits to be processed, making your blood alcohol concentration rise. This is what makes you feel drunk. Here are some common symptoms you might experience as your BAC rises:

- At a BAC of 0.02, you might feel relaxed, maybe a little lightheaded, and less inhibited.

- At a BAC of 0.05, your reaction times are slower (making it dangerous to drive), your emotions may become more exaggerated, and you probably feel a "buzz."

---

[*] Women, for many reasons, tend to get drunk more quickly and feel the effects of alcohol more intensely than men. This is in part because women are typically smaller in stature and have a smaller volume of blood than men. Women also have less water in their bodies and a higher proportion of body fat than men do, which both affect how the body processes alcohol.

- At a BAC of 0.08, your ability to drive is very impaired, you may start to slur your words, you may start to stumble, and you probably don't realize how drunk you are.

- At a BAC of 0.20, you may stumble, get confused, vomit, or black out (lose consciousness). You can die by choking on your own vomit.

- At a BAC of 0.30, you may be in a daze, having no idea where you are or what you are doing. Death can occur at this level.

- At a BAC of 0.40, you may slip into a coma and your risk of death is high since you may stop breathing or your heart may stop beating.

You can find BAC tables online to get an estimate of how much alcohol it takes to reach various blood alcohol concentrations. For example, a 120-pound woman can drink only two drinks in an hour before reaching a 0.08 BAC, while a 180-pound man can have four drinks before his BAC rises to 0.08. Keep in mind that these are just estimates. If you are having mixed drinks, you probably don't know exactly how much alcohol is in the drink or how strong the alcohol is. This makes it easier to get drunk, since you might not realize how much you've had.

Race and ethnicity are also factors when considering your BAC. For example, Asians and Native Americans tend to process alcohol slowly, so their BAC rises fast. They get drunk quickly and with less alcohol.

> **Keep Track of Your BAC** ⚡TIP!
>
> Alcohol.org has a free BAC calculator you can use to get an idea of how intoxicated you might be based on your weight, sex, and how many drinks you've had. You can also download apps for your phone. Some free apps include iDrinkSmarter, AlcoDroid Alcohol Tracker, and Alcohol Check. Many more are available.

Reasons People Use Alcohol

Though we often refer to "drugs and alcohol," alcohol is actually a drug, since it has a number of qualities that affect a person's mood and behavior. And it is one of the most commonly abused substances in the world by people of all ages, partly because it is legal for adults to drink. Many people use alcohol to relax or boost their mood. Other people use it to relieve anxiety. If you are nervous around others, say at a party where you don't know many people, alcohol can make it easier to talk with people you don't know. If you're relaxed, others may think you're more interesting and fun to be around.

Some teens use alcohol to get drunk with friends. Stumbling around and saying or doing silly things can be fun. Talking about how drunk you got can also give you bragging rights with friends the next day.

Others drink because they like the taste. Wine coolers and canned cocktails often come in fruity flavors. Beer comes in many different varieties. Hard liquors such as vodka, rum, whiskey, and gin can be mixed with other drinks, such as tonic water, soda, or juice. Some people drink shots of liquor instead of mixing it. Drinking games such as beer pong and quarters are common on college campuses.

For ideas on how to feel good without using drugs or alcohol, see the sidebar on page 17. Chapter 7 also shares ways to help you avoid the urge to drink.

Risks of Using Alcohol

Using alcohol as a teen can affect how your brain develops. Alcohol can make it harder for you to learn and remember, and using it as a teen increases your likelihood of developing a substance use problem. (For a list of signs you or someone you know may have a substance use problem, see page 12 in chapter 1.) According to the National Institute on Alcohol Abuse and

Alcoholism (NIAAA), people who start drinking at an early age, before age 17, are much more likely to become addicted than people who wait until they are older.

Getting drunk makes it harder to make good decisions too. You are more likely to take risks, such as driving while drunk, or lose control over your feelings and actions. You might hurt someone when you get mad. If you are too drunk to realize the other person isn't interested, you could sexually assault someone. And if you pass out, you could be sexually assaulted and not even remember what happened. You're also more likely to attempt suicide when you drink, since alcohol makes depression worse for many people.

Drinking too much can also kill you. You may get sleepy and pass out. You could develop alcohol poisoning, which affects your breathing and your heart rate and can cause permanent brain damage. Drinking games may seem like fun, but they greatly increase the chances of alcohol poisoning because of how fast

Keep Yourself Safe

If you drink at a party or club, keep an eye on your drink at all times, especially if you don't know everyone well. Some people will spike others' drinks with drugs known as date-rape drugs so they can commit sexual assault. You may not even remember it happened when you wake up.

and how much you drink. You could choke on your own vomit or stop breathing. Some people black out, meaning that they don't have any memory of what they did while they were drunk.

Drinking hard liquor (vodka, rum, tequila, whiskey) is generally more dangerous than drinking beer or wine since liquors contain a higher percentage of alcohol. This means that even small amounts of liquor can get you drunk quickly. Most people who die of alcohol poisoning die from drinking too much liquor. Even if you pass out, the level of alcohol in your body (your BAC) can continue to rise, increasing your risk of death.

Drinking too much beer or wine can still harm you, though. For example, chugging or shotgunning a beer, which involves drinking a can or glass of beer as fast as possible, is dangerous because of how quickly the alcohol can build up in your body.

HELPING FRIENDS WITH ALCOHOL POISONING

If you drink with your friends, chances are that at some point, one of your friends will drink too much. Signs that someone has had too much alcohol include confusion, vomiting, passing out, trouble breathing, cold and clammy skin, low body temperature, seizures, and slowed heart rate.

If you see someone with these symptoms, call 911 immediately! Don't try to sober them up with coffee, food, or a cold shower. This can make it worse. Don't worry about getting in trouble—saving someone's life is always more important. And never leave the person alone to sleep it off or wait for them to sober up. Young people have died when their friends and fellow students left them alone after a night of heavy drinking. Some of these classmates are serving jail time for not taking appropriate action (calling 911) that could have saved someone's life. For more information about alcohol poisoning, visit teens.drugabuse.gov/drug-facts/alcohol.

Each year, almost 2,000 people under age 21 die in car crashes in which alcohol use is a factor. In fact, alcohol is involved in nearly half of all violent deaths involving young people. People who are intoxicated may feel confident in their ability to drive, but the reality is that it doesn't take much alcohol to affect your driving skills—even just one drink can increase your risk of an accident. This is why teens and young adults under age 21 can be arrested for driving with any amount of alcohol in their bloodstream. Alcohol makes your reaction times slower, makes it harder to see and hear accurately, and makes it harder to focus on driving. You might take risks you would not ordinarily take if you were sober too. For example, according to the CDC, in 2017, 58 percent of teen drivers killed in car crashes after drinking and driving were not wearing a seat belt.

Some parents let their teens drink at home, even with friends. They think that if everyone stays at their house, or if they supervise the drinking, it's safer than teens going out and drinking. That may be true. However, parents can't legally allow other underage teens to drink in their home. A number of parents have been arrested, and have even served time in jail, for doing this. If someone at your house leaves drunk and gets into an accident on the way home, your parents or guardians can be held responsible. They can be sued.

Heavy alcohol use also leads to problems later in life. Scientists have tools to measure how alcohol and other drugs affect the brain, and your brain actually shrinks when you drink heavily. Most of the shrinking happens in the frontal lobe, which handles your ability to think, make decisions, and control impulses. Your hippocampus, the part of the brain that helps you remember things, can shrink too. Your risk for developing dementia later in life also increases.

There are at least 40 different neurotransmitter systems in the brain that are affected by long-term alcohol abuse. (Neurotransmitters are chemicals your nerve cells use to communicate with each other.) For example, dopamine is a neurotransmitter that helps people focus and makes activities more pleasurable. Most abusable drugs, including alcohol, cause a powerful surge of dopamine—that's what gives you the high feeling. When these drugs wear off, dopamine levels fall, which can make you feel worse than you did before using. Over time, it can become much harder for the brain to experience pleasure without using alcohol or other drugs. This damage to the brain is partly why alcoholics have such a hard time stopping.

A recent study led by researcher John Peyton Bohnsack found that teens who start abusing alcohol before age 21 have changes in the part of the brain known as the amygdala. The amygdala is involved in the fight-or-flight response your brain has when it thinks that you're in danger. Changes in the amygdala can make you more emotionally reactive, more likely to take risks, and more likely to develop mental health problems when you're older.

Another risk of alcohol use is the risk of pregnancy. Drinking may lead you to make risky decisions about sex, such as having unprotected sex, that you wouldn't make when you are sober. And if you are pregnant, alcohol (and drug) use during pregnancy is extremely harmful to the fetus. It can lead to fetal alcohol syndrome (FAS), which causes brain damage and growth problems in children. Children with FAS typically suffer from attention problems, intellectual disability, impaired memory, heart defects, and much more. If you're not trying to get pregnant, you might not realize at first that you are and may continue to drink or use drugs in the early weeks and months of your pregnancy.

Drinking Responsibly

The safest approach is to not drink at all. You will never become an alcoholic if you choose not to drink. But if you do drink, it is important to drink responsibly. Here are some ways you can reduce the harm that comes from drinking.

Pace yourself. Remember, your body can only process about one regular drink (see page 22) an hour. When you drink more than that, alcohol backs up in your bloodstream, raising your BAC. The more you drink and the faster you drink, the more risks you take. If you keep yourself to having one or two drinks an hour, you are less likely to pass out or lose control of yourself.

Use a BAC calculator to give you a rough idea of how fast your blood alcohol concentration is rising. This may help you slow down if you realize that it is getting too high. You can even purchase handheld blood alcohol devices. Remember, no amount of alcohol in your bloodstream is legal when you are under 21.

Never drink and drive. Always have a designated driver who won't drink, or drink somewhere where no one has to drive. Call a cab or get a rideshare (like an Uber or Lyft) if you are too drunk to drive. If you take an Uber or Lyft, always check the license plate number and the make and model of the car to make sure they match up with the information in your app. And ask the driver who they are picking up before you get in the car. You can ask your parents or guardians if they'd be willing to set up a rideshare account for you so you'll always have money to get yourself home.

Don't let your friends drive if they have been drinking, and don't get in a car with someone who has been drinking. Take their keys if necessary. Looking out for your friends is part of being a good friend, even if they get mad at you in the moment. Many drunk driving accidents happen within a few miles of a person's home.

DON'T DRINK AND DRIVE

In the United States, the legal blood alcohol limit for adults over 21 is 0.08 percent. As few as two drinks in an hour can put you over that limit. People under age 21 can be arrested and charged with driving under the influence (DUI) if you have *any* alcohol in your system. Even if you are 21 or older, you can be charged with a DUI when your blood alcohol level is below the legal limit if you are stopped by the police and the officer arresting you believes that alcohol was a factor in how you were driving (too fast, too slow, or swerving in the road) or if you get into an accident. Don't take a chance. Make arrangements ahead of time so you are not tempted to drink and drive.

Eat before and during the time you are drinking. This helps your body absorb alcohol more slowly.

Alternate between alcoholic and nonalcoholic beverages. Having water and other nonalcoholic liquids between drinks can slow down your alcohol intake and can help your liver and kidneys metabolize and detoxify alcohol in your bloodstream. However, drinking water between alcoholic drinks will *not* keep you from getting drunk or from experiencing the negative effects of having too much too quickly.

While these suggestions can lower your risk of dangerous consequences of using alcohol, this doesn't mean that drinking alcohol is a safe choice. You may have the best intentions, but when you're around your friends, it can be harder to stick with what you know is the best approach.

Moderation Management

You might also consider learning to manage your drinking behavior. Some people have an alcohol addiction, but once they accept that it is a problem, they are able to control it so that it doesn't cause issues with their school, relationships, and work. The group Moderation Management is designed to help people take control over their behavior, whether they choose to abstain completely from alcohol or try to control their use by setting safer limits. They offer support groups and online resources to help people take responsibility for setting and meeting their own behavior goals. However, they strongly recommend 30 days of abstinence first—that is, no drinking (or using other drugs) at all for that period of time. If you can't go that long, chances are that moderating your drinking isn't for you. For more information, check out their website moderation.org.

Drinking is part of life for many people. Since it is legal for adults over 21, it's easy to downplay some of the serious problems that alcohol use can cause. By understanding the risks involved, you can make smarter choices about your own use of alcohol. If you think your alcohol use or someone else's is a problem, chapters 6 and 7 share ways to help you overcome your addiction and say no to the urge to drink.

CHAPTER 3

Drug Use— Just the Facts

"I'd never do harder drugs, and I don't consider marijuana to be a drug."

• • • •

"I didn't think I'd like to trip on acid, but it was one of the best experiences of my life. I feel like I got closer to the universe and that everything started making sense."

• • • •

"I took Adderall from a friend because I heard it can help you do better studying for tests. I did remember more stuff, but I couldn't fall asleep until three a.m. Then I started hallucinating—seeing things and hearing voices calling my name. It freaked me out."

Drugs have been around for thousands of years. Humans have always looked for ways to feel better, whether to have fun, deal with boredom, have mystical experiences, relieve pain, or cope with other problems. And people are still searching to find drugs that help people feel better without causing problems or side effects—think medications. However, all drugs, both prescription and illegal, have side effects, some of them deadly. In this chapter, you'll learn about the various drugs of abuse, including prescription drugs, and some of the problems that can go along with using them.

What Is a Drug?

A drug is any substance that when taken (by swallowing it in a pill or as a liquid, smoking it, vaping it, sniffing it, or injecting it into your veins, among other ways) causes one or more physical or psychological effects. This includes alcohol, nicotine, caffeine, and other legal drugs, as well as marijuana, acid, cocaine, and other illegal drugs. Medications used to treat a headache or illnesses are drugs, but most are not abused. Most antidepressant drugs (such as Prozac, Zoloft, and Lexapro) are not abused because they take weeks to start working; you don't feel anything the same day you first take them, and most drug users want to feel better immediately. However, antianxiety medications, such as Xanax and Valium, are more likely to be abused because they work quickly and because taking more than the recommended dose can get you high. Painkillers such as Vicodin, Percocet, and OxyContin are similarly prone to abuse. For this chapter, we are focused on drugs that people can abuse.

Drugs interfere with the way your nerve cells (called neurons) communicate with one another. Some drugs can activate neurons because their structure is similar to natural brain chemicals called neurotransmitters. These drugs make your neurons release large quantities of neurotransmitters, overloading your brain. Many drugs, including nicotine, cause the release of the neurotransmitter dopamine, which makes you enjoy activities or can make you feel energized.

GENERIC VS. BRAND-NAME MEDICATIONS

When a new drug comes out, the company that makes it has a patent on it. This means that no other company can make the same drug, usually for about 20 years. After that, other companies can make the drug; these are called generics and are cheaper than the brand-name drug. For example, the antianxiety drug Valium can be purchased as the generic drug diazepam. The generic form of Ritalin is methylphenidate. In this chapter, you'll often see the name of a brand-name prescription drug followed by its generic name in parentheses. Brand-name drugs and generics generally are equally effective.

What Is Drug Abuse?

Abusing a drug means taking an illegal drug or taking more than the recommended dose of a prescription drug to feel better physically or emotionally or to get high. (For a list of signs you or someone you know may have a substance use problem, see page 12 in chapter 1.) For example, the drug OxyContin (oxycodone) is a pain reliever, which works quite well at the recommended amount. However, taking more than this amount (a form of overdosing) can give users a high and a sense of relief from emotional pain. Cough syrups, such as codeine or those that contain DXM (dextromethorphan), work well if you have a cough. Overdosing on them can also create a high.

Another type of drug abuse is taking a medication not prescribed for you. For example, the stimulant drugs Ritalin, Concerta (methylphenidate hydrochloride), Adderall (amphetamine/dextroamphetamine), Focalin (dexmethylphenidate), and Vyvanse (lisdexamfetamine) are some of the medications used to treat ADHD. They are used with a prescription to help people diagnosed with ADHD focus better. But if someone who doesn't need them takes these drugs, they can make the user hyper or keep them up all night. Many college students abuse Adderall and other stimulants to stay awake. They may get them from friends who are prescribed these medications. In larger doses, these medications can get you high—they can improve your mood and make you feel like you can accomplish anything. But higher doses can also kill you by making your heart stop.

If you are concerned about your use of drugs or someone else's, chapters 6 and 7 share ways to help you overcome your addiction and prevent relapse. And for ideas to help you feel good without using drugs or alcohol, see the sidebar on page 17.

Types of Drugs People Abuse

Many drugs can be abused. (For more about substance use problems, see chapter 1.) Most fall into one of four classifications: depressants, narcotics, stimulants, and hallucinogens. The National Institute on Drug Abuse (NIDA) has an excellent website that lists 29 different substances that are commonly abused. Check out their site if you want more information: drugabuse.gov /drug-topics/commonly-abused-drugs-charts.

1. **Depressants:** Also called tranquilizers, these drugs slow the activity of your brain and nerves, which has a calming effect. They are often used to lower anxiety and help people sleep. Examples include a type of drug known as benzodiazepines, such as Valium (diazepam), Ativan (lorazepam), Xanax (alprazolam), and Klonopin (clonazepam). Benzodiazepines can also help relieve muscle tension. Many are used to prevent seizures when taken on a regular basis. Ironically, though, people who don't suffer from seizures but who abuse these drugs can experience withdrawal seizures when they stop using because their bodies have become dependent on the drug. (These kinds of seizures can also happen when a person is withdrawing from regular alcohol use.) Because benzodiazepines work quickly, they can be more addictive than other depressant drugs. BuSpar (buspirone) is a depressant that is used to treat anxiety. It is milder than

benzodiazepines, takes longer to work, and is, therefore, less likely to be addictive.

2. **Narcotics (opioids and painkillers):** Narcotics, or opioids, act on the opioid receptors in the brain and are used to relieve pain or reduce coughing. Naturally derived narcotic drugs are made from the opium poppy. Examples include morphine, heroin, codeine, Vicodin (hydrocodone/acetaminophen), and OxyContin. These drugs can be helpful for severe pain and may be prescribed after surgery or for a sports injury. Synthetic versions of these drugs (those made in a laboratory) are also available. Fentanyl is an example of a manufactured opioid. In addition to relieving pain, narcotics can make people feel very relaxed and happy. Some people are genetically predisposed to these mood changes from narcotics.

3. **Stimulants:** These drugs can give you energy and improve your focus. Commonly prescribed for people with ADHD, these medications stimulate the control centers of the brain, making people less hyperactive and more focused. Stimulants increase levels of dopamine in the brain, which makes activities more pleasurable. Examples include Ritalin, Adderall, cocaine, crystal meth, and ecstasy (methylenedioxymethamphetamine, also known as MDMA). Caffeine is also a stimulant, but it is generally not abused. Bath salts (cathinones) are also stimulant drugs.

4. **Hallucinogens (psychedelics):** These drugs alter your perception of reality. They can make you see or hear things that aren't there. Examples include LSD (lysergic acid diethylamide), PCP (phencyclidine), peyote (mescaline), ketamine, and magic mushrooms. Marijuana is another example of a hallucinogen, though this depends on the type and amount you use. Hallucinogens can increase your heart rate, make your senses more intense, and make time seem to pass more slowly. While hallucinogens are not generally

physically dangerous, they can cause you to have a bad trip, which can last for hours. A bad trip occurs when your hallucinations are frightening; you may think others are trying to attack you, think you are going crazy, or have other nightmarish visions. You can also have flashbacks, meaning that the symptoms of your bad trip come back in the future, without warning. It can happen days, weeks, or even years after using hallucinogenic drugs, though not everyone experiences this. Another danger of taking these drugs is that you may do things that could kill you. For example, you might believe you can fly and jump out of a window.

Many drugs have multiple effects. For example, marijuana in small doses can have a calming effect or help you sleep, so it acts as a depressant. In large amounts, you might hallucinate, become paranoid (thinking others are out to get you), or lose touch with reality—in these ways, marijuana acts as a hallucinogen. Marijuana can also be used to relieve pain, so it acts like a narcotic. Nicotine can make you feel energized (stimulant), but it also has a calming effect (depressant).

HALLUCINOGEN–PERSISTING PERCEPTION DISORDER

Hallucinogen-persisting perception disorder (HPPD) affects some users of hallucinogenic drugs. You can experience flashbacks that include hallucinations or other visual disturbances, such as seeing "visual snow" or what appears as dots or lines. You can also see trails when objects move. These visual effects happen without warning a few days or even a year or more after drug use. HPPD symptoms are similar to those caused by other brain problems, such as tumors or strokes. HPPD occurs more often in people who have a history of mental illness, but it can happen to anyone, even after using hallucinogens only one time. Though rare, HPPD can last for years. While there are medications that can help, if you experience symptoms, continued drug use is much riskier and should be avoided.

ARE ENERGY DRINKS OKAY?

Energy drinks are popular with teens and adults. According to the National Center for Complementary and Integrative Health (NCCIH), about a third of all teens in the United States report using them regularly. Energy drinks contain stimulants such as caffeine and additives such as ginseng, guarana, yohimbe, carnitine, and sugar. Since many teens don't get enough sleep and have to wake up early for school, they might think energy drinks are a harmless way to wake up and get through the day. But these drinks can make your heart race, increase your blood pressure, interfere with sleep, and cause weight gain. Mixing energy drinks with alcohol is especially dangerous. Teens who use both are four times as likely to binge drink, since energy drinks also make it harder to tell how drunk and impaired you are. In some cases, people have had to go to the emergency room after using energy drinks, especially if they combined them with alcohol, drugs, or prescription medications.

Specific Drugs People Abuse

Some of the most commonly abused illegal and prescription drugs and important facts you should know about them are described next, in alphabetical order. For more information about specific drugs of abuse, the NIDA website is an excellent resource. Visit drugabuse.gov / drug-topics. To read about alcohol use, see chapter 2.

Bath Salts

Cathinone is a natural stimulant found in the khat plant native to Africa and Arabia. Synthetic (made in a lab) cathinones are sold as bath salts. Street names include Bloom, Cloud Nine, Cosmic Blast, Ivory Wave, Lunar Wave, Scarface, Vanilla Sky, and White Lightning. The chemical makeup of these drugs is similar to that of other stimulants, such as meth and ecstasy. However, synthetic cathinones are much stronger and more dangerous than the naturally occurring substance. Bath salts are often sold as other products to disguise the fact that they are actually illegal drugs.

They look like a white or brown crystal-like powder and are sold in small packets. (Note: Actual bath salts, such as Epsom salts, are not drugs.) People use this drug by sniffing, swallowing, or injecting it. While bath salts can make people feel happier and more social, they can also cause paranoia, hallucinations, rapid heart rate, muscle spasms, anxiety, kidney failure, and seizures. Swallowing bath salts causes a peak "rush" in about 90 minutes. The effects can last for three or four hours, followed by a crash. The total experience can last up to eight hours. Snorting and injecting the drug are especially dangerous.

Cocaine

Cocaine is a stimulant drug. It is a white powder that is made from the leaves of the coca plant and has been used for thousands of years. It can give people energy and allow them to stay awake for hours without sleeping. Cocaine can make you feel revved up and energized, more confident, and more talkative. It makes your heart beat faster and raises your blood pressure. People can sniff cocaine, smoke it in a pipe, or use a needle to give themselves a shot. This is called shooting up.

Crack cocaine is a type of cocaine that is mixed with baking soda or ammonia and water. Once it dries, it is cut into chunks called rocks. A crack cocaine user puts the rock into a pipe and smokes it. This is called freebasing. Crack cocaine is one of the most addictive drugs around. People can get addicted after using only a few times.

The effects of cocaine last only a short time. When it wears off, you may feel depressed, anxious, and tired. People who are addicted to cocaine want to use more to feel good again. They also have cravings—strong desires to use the drug again. This makes it very addictive.

Using cocaine is very dangerous. It can cause heart attacks or strokes. Sniffing or snorting it can cause nosebleeds and damage the nose. Overdosing (OD-ing) on cocaine can kill you. If you share needles with other users, you could contract HIV/AIDS or a life-threatening blood infection. Frequent use of cocaine can also cause kidney failure.

Cough Syrup (DXM)

Some people drink large amounts of cough syrup containing DXM to get high. This is sometimes called robotripping. They will drink most or all of a bottle, which is a form of overdosing because they are taking much more than the recommended dose for a cough. Because cough syrup is sold in stores, you might think it is safe to take more than is recommended. However, overdosing on cough syrup can make you feel dizzy or numb and lose your balance. It can give you a buzz or high similar to PCP. Some people report having an out-of-body experience while using it. Using cough syrup to get high is dangerous because it can cause high blood pressure, make your heart beat faster, damage your liver, and cause you to lose control of your muscles. It can even lead to seizures, coma, and permanent brain damage. You can overheat if you take it and then exercise or go to a club and dance. Some people die from drinking too much cough syrup. Most drugstores now keep this medication behind the counter to make it harder for people to buy it.

Crystal Meth

Crystal methamphetamine, also called crystal meth or Ice, is a stimulant drug similar to cocaine. It gives people lots of energy and makes them feel very happy and excited, at least at first. This drug is popular in dance clubs and bars because it gives people enough energy to dance all night. It comes in chunky clear crystals and is usually smoked, though it can be crushed to sniff or injected using a needle. It is highly addictive, can cause damage to your brain and heart, and can kill you.

DMT

Dimethyltryptamine (DMT or N,N-DMT) is a psychedelic drug that can cause intense hallucinations. Ayahuasca is an herbal drink or tea that contains DMT and is made from plants that grow in the Amazon jungle. It has been used for hundreds of years and is thought to have spiritual and therapeutic benefits. This drink is illegal in the United States. Side effects include vomiting, diarrhea, elevated blood pressure, and a rapid heart rate.

Ecstasy

MDMA, also known as ecstasy or E, is another stimulant drug, though it also has hallucinogenic effects (see Hallucinogens on page 35). It comes in tablets or capsules, and its effects last about four to six hours. People who use this drug feel happier and more peaceful, and want to get physically closer to others. Negative effects include muscle aches, chills and sweating, teeth clenching, trouble concentrating or remembering things, a rapid heart rate, confusion, trouble sleeping, and paranoia. People often use ecstasy at dance clubs and may dance all night, which can be especially dangerous if they don't drink enough water. Ecstasy can also cause liver damage, heart attacks, and seizures. You can die from overdosing on it.

Fentanyl

This is a synthetic (made in a laboratory) opioid, or narcotic, drug that is similar to heroin—only it's 50 times more powerful. Fentanyl is prescribed to relieve pain, and often comes as a skin patch for people with moderate to severe pain who need relief 24 hours a day. When prescribed, this drug is known as Actiq, Duragesic, and Sublimaze. Street names for fentanyl, or for fentanyl-laced heroin, include Apache, China Girl, China White, Dance Fever, Friend, Goodfella, Jackpot, Murder 8, TNT, and Tango and Cash.

Fentanyl is extremely dangerous since it is very easy to overdose on it. When abused, it usually is made as a powder or a liquid that can be dropped onto paper or is made into pills. Some dealers mix it into other drugs such as heroin or meth to make those drugs more powerful. However, when users buy drugs cut with fentanyl, they can never know exactly how strong the drugs are, which is why so many people overdose on fentanyl.

Carfentanil is an even more dangerous drug. This opioid is 10,000 times more potent than morphine and 100 times more potent than fentanyl and is used by veterinarians to sedate large animals. It is a very powerful pain reliever. As with fentanyl, people sell carfentanil instead of heroin (or add it to heroin) because it's cheaper since it is so much more powerful. That also makes it more deadly; it takes very little carfentanil to kill a person. When veterinarians use it, they wear protective gear to make sure that they don't get any on their skin or breathe it in.

GHB

Gamma hydroxybutyrate (GHB) is a depressant drug that goes by various names: Easy Lay, Georgia Home Boy, Liquid X or Liquid Ecstasy, and Gamma-OH. It usually comes in a liquid (which may taste soapy or salty) and may be used by bodybuilders as a supplement to build muscle or reduce fat. It is also used to treat narcolepsy, which causes excessive sleepiness during the day. GHB is perhaps best known as a date-rape drug. It can be added to a drink to sedate someone to the point where they cannot react if someone tries to have sex with them. Effects begin quickly and can last for hours. GHB can make you feel very happy and increase your sex drive. You may develop tolerance and experience withdrawal symptoms if you stop using it. It can make you sweat, give you nausea, and make you hallucinate. It can slow your breathing, which increases your risk for death. GHB is especially dangerous when mixed with alcohol.

Heroin

Heroin, also called Junk or Smack, is an opioid drug. Heroin is a powder that can be white or brown. It is usually heated until it turns into a liquid and then put into a syringe. A person injects the shot of heroin directly into a vein. The effects last a few hours, and the user may look sleepy—a state that is called nodding out. Then the user needs another shot to avoid going into withdrawal, which is often painful. A heroin addict is sometimes called a junkie. Some people inhale or sniff heroin instead.

Heroin slows down your breathing and makes you constipated. People can overdose and die if they use too much. Once someone starts using heroin, especially by injecting it, it's very difficult to stop—it might even feel impossible. Heroin is one of the most highly addictive drugs. People feel happy and calm while using it but get depressed and anxious when it wears off. Stopping heroin use can be very painful, since your body loses its natural ability to control pain when you take heroin or other opioids on a regular basis. Some people say that the first time they got high on heroin is the best they have ever felt. Each subsequent time they use, they hope to feel that good again, but never do. This is called chasing the high. People can be addicted to heroin for many years. Using a needle that isn't clean can spread diseases such as hepatitis and HIV/AIDS, as well as cause life-threatening bacterial blood infections.

Heroin and other opioids are dangerous drugs. An overdose can kill you by stopping your breathing. It can happen as soon as 20 minutes or as long as two hours after using. Signs that someone has overdosed include unresponsiveness, loss of color in the face and clammy skin, fingertips and lips turning blue, slow or erratic breathing (or stopped breathing), a loud snoring or gurgling sound, and a slow or stopped heartbeat.

AN OVERDOSE IS ALWAYS AN EMERGENCY

If you are with someone and see signs of a possible overdose, call 911 immediately. Paramedics can use a drug called Narcan (naloxone) that reverses the effects of the overdose. It can be given using a syringe or as a nasal spray. But it must be done quickly to keep someone from dying. Naloxone auto-injectors you can use on yourself (or someone else) in the event of an overdose are available, but they are very expensive and must be prescribed. They're about the size of a box of Tic Tacs and contain a retractable needle.

Inhalants

Inhalants are chemicals that people inhale to get high. This is known as sniffing (if inhaled through the nose) or huffing (if inhaled through the mouth). *Bagging* is a slang term, which refers to spraying the chemical into a bag and inhaling from the bag. Hundreds of chemicals can be used as inhalants, including solvents (such as paint thinner), gasoline, nail polish, permanent markers, and model glue, among many others. Inhalants also include aerosols (chemicals that are sprayed out of cans), such as hair spray, deodorant, and spray paint.

Nitrites are another type of inhalant. They usually come in small brown jars and are known as Poppers or Snappers. These chemicals can make you feel high or drunk for a short time, usually about 15 to 30 minutes. You may feel lightheaded and less inhibited. Some people use nitrites to make sexual activity more intense.

After using inhalants, you may feel numb, dizzy, tired, and confused. Inhalants can also cause hallucinations. Some people experience nosebleeds. Over time, inhalants can make you feel unmotivated, cause sores in your mouth or around your lips, and make you stop caring about your appearance. Inhalants are toxic chemicals—they are very dangerous. It is hard to control how much you inhale. They can cause brain damage, heart attacks, kidney failure, hearing loss, and death.

Ketamine

Ketamine (also known as Special K or Vitamin K) is a hallucinogenic drug that was originally used as an anesthetic in veterinary medicine. It is available as a liquid or a white powder. Ketamine can be injected, snorted, smoked (by adding the powder to tobacco or marijuana cigarettes), or swallowed. Ketamine can cause problems with attention, learning, and memory. It can also cause hallucinations, sedation, and confusion. It can make you feel detached from your body and can raise your blood pressure, make you lose consciousness, or slow your breathing. You can die from ketamine abuse, since it can affect your ability to clear your throat, causing you to choke.

Ketamine is also used as a date-rape drug. It can make you hallucinate and unable to move so that you can't physically stop someone who is sexually assaulting you. You may not even remember being assaulted.

More recently, ketamine is being used as a therapy for severe depression. It is usually given as a nasal spray and works fast, but this treatment *must* be done in a controlled setting so that medical staff can observe you for a few hours in case you have a bad reaction.

LSD

One of the original hallucinogens is LSD, commonly called acid. LSD is made in laboratories. It is a liquid that has no odor, color, or taste. Often, it is placed on sheets of paper that look like stamps, and people lick the paper to get high. Sometimes LSD is made into colorful pills. The effects of LSD can last six to nine hours and can change your sense of time, place, and reality.

Physical effects can include stomach upset, dizziness, enlarged pupils, muscle weakness, loss of appetite, trouble sleeping, and increased blood pressure. LSD can also make you see things that are not real. Some people report seeing sounds or tasting colors because their senses get mixed up—this is called synesthesia. It can be a fun experience for some. For others, however, the effects of LSD can be very scary—this is called a bad trip. During a bad trip, you may panic and become very anxious. You can have bad trips long after you stop using LSD too. These are called flashbacks. Some people develop serious mental or emotional problems after using LSD.

MICRODOSING

Some teens "microdose" hallucinogenic drugs such as LSD or mushrooms containing psilocybin. Microdosing is when people take a small amount of the drug, rather than a typical dose. James Fadiman, author of the 2011 book *The Psychedelic Explorer's Guide*, described the concept of microdosing. To microdose, a person takes roughly one-tenth of a trip-inducing dose every three or four days. Some people report that microdosing improves their mood, lowers their anxiety, helps them gain insight, and facilitates creative thinking. Some studies support microdosing when it is done under the supervision and guidance of a medical professional. However, not all medical professionals support its use. Any drug use has the potential for addiction and other dangerous consequences. It is difficult to do large-scale studies of hallucinogenic drugs, since they are illegal to buy, sell, and use. This makes it hard to know for sure what the risks and benefits are.

Marijuana (Natural)

Marijuana (cannabis), also called dope, pot, or weed, is one of the most commonly abused drugs of all the drugs mentioned in this chapter. It comes from a type of cannabis plant and has been around for over 4,000 years. It looks like dried green or brown leaves and may include seeds and stems. The active ingredient in marijuana is called THC (tetrahydrocannabinol). The more THC in the marijuana, the stronger the effect it has. Marijuana is often smoked in a rolled cigarette, called a joint. Some people remove the tobacco from a cigar and replace it with marijuana—this is called a blunt. Others smoke marijuana using a bowl (a small pipe) or a bong (a larger pipe that filters the smoke through water). Sometimes marijuana is added to foods such as brownies and eaten. These are called edibles.

As with many drugs, people use marijuana to relax and cope with problems. Marijuana might cause feelings of anger to go away and may make you laugh over nothing. It can also help you sleep and reduce pain, so it is sometimes prescribed for medical uses (see page 57). Different strains of marijuana do different things in the body.

Marijuana has all kinds of effects on the body and brain. The human body produces chemicals called endocannabinoids, which are neurotransmitters that work on the nervous systems. The THC in marijuana activates those same nerve cells, which is how it produces its effects. Marijuana can make it harder to keep your balance and can slow your reaction times, making it dangerous to drive. The senses, such as touch, vision, and hearing, can become more intense. Time might seem to pass more slowly. Marijuana can make you feel hungry, and it can be harder for you to make positive choices when you're high. You might forget what you're talking about, even in the middle of a sentence.

DON'T SMOKE AND DRIVE

Marijuana significantly affects your judgment, motor coordination, and reaction time, and it impairs your ability to drive. This effect increases the higher the level of THC in your blood. Marijuana is the drug most often found in the blood of drivers who have been involved in car accidents, especially ones that result in death. Having THC in your blood makes you twice as likely to cause a fatal car accident, and three to seven times more likely to have caused an accident, especially if alcohol is also involved.*

Marijuana can make some people paranoid, which means they think that others are out to get them. Smoking a lot of marijuana can make you hallucinate (see or hear things that aren't really there). Some people develop amotivational syndrome, which means that they don't feel motivated to do much of anything. Marijuana also makes it harder to

---

* For more information about the effects of marijuana on driving, see drugabuse.gov /publications/research-reports/marijuana/does-marijuana-use-affect-driving.

concentrate and to remember things. This often causes a drop in grades at school. Finally, smoking marijuana may cause cancer.

Some people believe that marijuana isn't addictive, especially with more states legalizing it for adult use. However, this is not true. Marijuana contains over 250 chemicals. The most well-known active ingredient is THC. This chemical can stay in your fat cells for over a month after you stop. While not everyone experiences withdrawal symptoms, others develop them within the first week of stopping marijuana use. Cravings can continue even longer. Typically, the more often you use, the more likely you are to experience withdrawal symptoms.

Here's something else to consider: heavy use of marijuana as a teen can greatly increase your risk for developing mental health disorders such as depression, bipolar disorder, or schizophrenia. This is especially true if you have family members with these disorders. While most marijuana users do not develop these disorders, it is clearly a risk to consider if you choose to use marijuana.

WHAT IS CBD OIL?

Cannabidiol (CBD) oil is a legal (in many but not all states) marijuana extract that is being sold as a drug that may ease pain, relieve anxiety, and improve sleep without getting people high. It is sold as gummies, gels, oils, and extracts. Since there are no regulations or standards for CBD products, there is no way of knowing if what you are buying actually works or what the right dose would be. More studies are needed. Some CBD products may have tiny amounts of THC.

For information about the legalization of marijuana for both recreational and medical uses, see the section Drugs and the Legal System on page 55.

Marijuana (Synthetic)

Some people use fake marijuana (also called synthetic marijuana) that is sold at gas stations and other places. Synthetic marijuana is often called Spice or K2. Other common names include Joker, Black Mamba, Kush, and Kronic. This drug is made of herbs and spices that are sprayed with chemicals. When smoked, it gives people a similar high to marijuana. People smoke K2 like marijuana, roll it into a blunt, or use a liquid form in an e-cigarette device. Synthetic marijuana is often labelled "not for human consumption," but that doesn't stop people from using it.

People who use synthetic marijuana think it is safe because it's legal. That's not true. The chemicals used, some of which are poisonous and illegal, are much stronger than what is usually found in marijuana. Manufacturers of synthetic marijuana keep changing the chemicals used in their products to avoid the law. Once one formula is made illegal, they try a slightly different version to get around the law. People have been sent to the emergency room after using synthetic marijuana with symptoms such as panic, paranoia, vomiting, suicidal thoughts, and violent behavior, among others. The chemicals used to make synthetic marijuana can kill you.

Mushrooms

Certain mushrooms, often called magic mushrooms or shrooms, are eaten to get high and feel relaxed. They can also be brewed as a tea or mixed in with other foods since they have a bitter taste. These mushrooms contain the drug psilocybin, which causes hallucinations. There is a long history between mushrooms and religious or spiritual ceremonies, dating as far back as 7,000 to 9,000 years. The Aztecs in Central America were known to use them. However, since some mushrooms are poisonous, and since it can be difficult to tell which mushrooms are poisonous, using mushrooms to get high can be dangerous. While mushrooms are not as addictive as many drugs, using them too often can make real life seem dull, which increases your risk for addiction. People who use mushrooms can also experience flashbacks.

PCP

PCP (phencyclidine), also known as Angel Dust, is a hallucinogenic drug that comes in a white powder that can be swallowed, smoked, sniffed, or injected using a needle. Sometimes it is sprayed onto leafy material, such as oregano, and smoked. It has a bitter taste when swallowed. It was developed as an anesthetic for use during surgery or other painful procedures in the 1950s, but this use ended when serious side effects occurred.

WET DRUGS

This refers to dipping tobacco or marijuana cigarettes in one or both of two substances: the hallucinogenic drug PCP and a formaldehyde-based embalming fluid. This was popular in the 1970s (often referred to as Loveboat) and is making a comeback. Combining these drugs is extremely risky and can cause problems such as scary hallucinations, paranoia, angry outbursts, depression, vomiting, vision problems, unconsciousness or coma, lung failure, brain damage, and death.

PCP increases your heart rate and can cause sweating, dizziness, and numbness. When someone takes a lot of PCP, they can experience sleepiness, convulsions, blurry vision, drooling, a flicking up and down of the eyes (nystagmus), and death.

PCP is also dangerous because it can cause violent or odd behavior in people who don't usually act that way. People may become fearful or anxious and hallucinate. PCP is sometimes added to marijuana, cocaine, or heroin, which is especially scary since people are not expecting to take PCP and are unprepared for its effects.

PCP is addictive and its use often leads to feeling like you need it to function, craving the drug, and desperately trying to get more. Using PCP over a long period of time can result in memory loss, trouble speaking and learning, depression, and weight loss.

Peyote

Peyote is a small cactus plant that contains the drug mescaline. Buttons (the crown or top of the cactus) are cut from the plant and dried. The dried buttons are eaten or soaked in water to make a tea. While peyote is sometimes used as a medicine, it is also used as a drug because it causes hallucinations similar to LSD. Some members of Native American tribes use it in religious ceremonies. They believe it makes it easier to communicate with a higher power. Risky side effects include high blood pressure, stomach upset, vomiting, and possible psychosis when used repeatedly.

Prescription Drugs

As described at the beginning of the chapter, prescription drugs can be abused. Narcotics such as OxyContin and Vicodin are given to people to relieve severe pain, such as pain that occurs after a back injury or a surgery. Other commonly abused prescription drugs include codeine, Valium, Percocet (oxycodone/acetaminophen), Percodan (aspirin/oxycodone), fentanyl (see page 40), and Dilaudid (hydromorphone).

Adderall is another commonly abused prescription drug. It is a stimulant medication (see page 35) that is used to treat symptoms of ADHD. Since it helps people focus (and stay awake when taken in higher doses), students sometimes abuse this drug to help them stay up all night to study for tests or complete other schoolwork. Adderall can curb your appetite, make you feel more irritable or anxious, cause your heart to beat rapidly, make you angry, and make your breathing rapid. In higher doses, and especially if used with alcohol, it can cause seizures, coma, or even death. Ritalin is another commonly abused stimulant medication prescribed for ADHD and has effects similar to Adderall.

Teens are more likely to abuse prescription drugs (or even sell them to get money for other drugs) because prescription drugs are commonly found in people's homes. Abusing these drugs is very addictive and can be deadly. You don't know how your body will react to a prescription drug that isn't yours, since the doctor who prescribed the drug doesn't know you. It is illegal to buy or sell drugs that were not prescribed for you, and it's also illegal to share your prescribed medications with friends. You can be charged with a crime if someone else is hurt or dies as a result.

A few years back, officials in the United States, concerned about people abusing prescription drugs (often opioids), started monitoring doctors who prescribed them. But as people found it more difficult to get these drugs from their doctors, they turned to illegal drugs, such as heroin, to support their habits.

Rohypnol

Rohypnol (flunitrazepam) is similar to Valium; it is a depressant drug and can be used to put people to sleep prior to surgery. Common names include roofies, Mind Erasers, and Mexican Valium. Rohypnol makes you sleepy and can relax your muscles. It can make you dizzy and forgetful. It is considered a date-rape drug because if someone slips a tablet in your drink, it can make you unconscious. Someone can sexually assault you without you knowing or even remembering. Rohypnol can slow your heart rate and breathing. When combined with alcohol, it can kill you.

Rohypnol was previously made as a white tablet that was odorless and colorless, making it easy to slip into someone's drink. It is now made as a light green oval pill with a blue core. When placed into a clear drink, it will turn the liquid blue, making it easier for people to identify it. However, generic pills may not have the blue dye. If you are at a party, it is important never to leave your drink unattended, especially if you don't know everyone there.

Steroids

Also known as Juice, roids, or Gym Candy, anabolic steroids are chemicals that are normally used to treat certain medical conditions, such as delayed puberty in male teenagers, osteoporosis, and endometriosis. (They are different from corticosteroids such as prednisone, which are used to treat medical conditions such as asthma, rashes, or Lupus.) Steroids can come in a pill or can be injected using a needle. People may use steroids to make their muscles grow bigger and stronger. Some bodybuilders and other athletes, such as wrestlers and football players, use steroids to improve their performance (called doping). Some people who aren't athletes use steroids to feel better about their bodies. Men use steroids more than women, since they are usually more interested in developing bigger muscles. Anabolic steroids are illegal to use without a prescription and using them is considered cheating by most sporting organizations.

Anabolic steroids are very addictive. People who try to stop using them may get depressed or feel very tired. Some people get very angry when using steroids. This is called roid rage. Steroids can damage your liver, increase your risk of heart or kidney disease, and make your hair fall out. They can affect the male sex organs by shrinking the testicles. Men who use steroids can develop breasts, known as gynecomastia. Steroids also suppress your immune system, making it harder to fight infections.

Tobacco and Nicotine

Tobacco is a plant with leaves that contain nicotine. The dried leaves can be smoked in cigarettes or a pipe, sniffed, or chewed. Chewing tobacco is called dipping. Cigarettes contain many chemicals. One of these is the drug nicotine. Nicotine helps you calm down and can make it easier to focus. It raises your blood pressure, breathing rate, and heart rate by triggering the release of the brain neurotransmitter epinephrine (also called adrenaline). It also boosts your mood by increasing the neurotransmitter dopamine.

Both cigarettes and chewing tobacco contain many other ingredients. When burned, cigarettes create more than 7,000 chemicals. At least 69 of these are known to cause cancer, and many are toxic. They include formaldehyde (embalming fluid), arsenic (used in rat poison), benzene (found in rubber cement and gasoline), butane (used in lighter fluid), cadmium (used in battery acid), and carbon monoxide.

CIGARETTES AND CANCER

How many cigarettes can you smoke without increasing your risk of cancer? We don't know for sure. Some scientists who study this believe that no amount of smoking is safe. But in general, the more cigarettes you smoke per day and the longer you smoke, the higher your risk of developing lung cancer and other diseases, including heart disease. And if you quit smoking cigarettes or dipping, the health benefits start immediately. Even after only one day without cigarettes, your blood pressure begins to drop, decreasing your risk for heart attack or heart disease. However, if you smoke for years and then quit, your risk for cancer is still higher than if you had never smoked at all. There are many free apps and calendars online that you can use to help you quit smoking.

While it usually does not cause behavior problems, using tobacco products for many years greatly increases your risk for cancer, lung disease, heart disease, dementia, Alzheimer's disease, and other physical problems. In the United States, smoking cigarettes causes about 80 to 90 percent of all cases of lung cancer. Cigarette smoking and dipping can cause cancer almost anywhere in the body, including in your mouth, throat, stomach, colon, rectum, liver, pancreas, kidney, bladder, and voice box (larynx). Even secondhand smoke can be damaging.

In pregnancy, smoking increases the chances for having a miscarriage or a stillbirth, and it increases the chances that the baby will have a low birth weight. You might not be thinking about that now, but if you are planning on having kids in the future, this is something to consider, since nicotine is incredibly addictive.

It is so addictive, in fact, that it is one of the hardest drugs to quit. Since it is illegal in the United States for people under 21 to buy tobacco products, bringing these products to school can result in suspension or other disciplinary action. Most smokers start when they are teens, so if you don't start when you are young, chances are you won't become a smoker. Medicines are available that can help you quit smoking, such as Nicorette gum, NicoDerm,

Chantix, and Zyban. While Nicorette gum and the NicoDerm patch both contain nicotine, the goal is to gradually lower the amount of nicotine you are using until you are able to quit, usually over a three-month period. While quitting smoking or dipping reduces your chances of getting cancer, your risk may not go back to that of someone who never used tobacco.

Vaping (Electronic Cigarettes)

Electronic cigarettes, commonly called e-cigarettes, have become popular with teens in recent years. You use a battery-operated device to vaporize a liquid (called e-juice or e-liquid) that contains nicotine and various other chemicals so you can breathe it into your lungs. E-liquid comes in pods that are placed into the device and is often flavored. Vaping is advertised as being safer than cigarettes because it doesn't contain the toxic chemicals found in cigarette smoke. It was initially marketed to customers as a safer way to consume nicotine and as an aide to cigarette smokers who wanted to quit. However, according to one 2019 study funded by the National Institute for Health Research and Cancer Research UK, about 80 percent of people who vaped to try to quit smoking were still smoking a year later. We don't know what the long-term effects of vaping are since these devices are so new. It was many years after cigarettes became popular before research showed how dangerous they were, something that the makers of tobacco products tried to hide from the public. Since e-cigarettes contain nicotine, they are highly addictive as well.

Federal and state health officials in the United States are currently investigating some of the more serious cases of illness related to vaping. As of February 2020, the CDC records that nearly 3,000 cases in all 50 states and two US territories have been reported, many involving teens and young adults. It is still unclear whether these illnesses are due to the vaping process or some of the ingredients used. E-liquids can contain nicotine, THC, CBD oil, flavorings, propylene glycol, glycerin, and other ingredients, according to the US Food and Drug Administration. By heating the liquid, e-cigarettes create an aerosol that contains very tiny and dangerous particles that can cause cancer.

While some e-cigarette companies have eliminated flavors popular with teens in response to concerns that they were marketing to teens, other companies have responded by increasing their selection of flavored pods. Some countries have made e-cigarettes illegal for adults, too, out of concern for people's health.

Another risk of vaping is that it increases the chances that you will go on to use marijuana. Teens who vape are 4.3 times more likely to use marijuana than teens who don't vape. And some people use e-cigarettes as a way of using marijuana. According to the CDC, these THC-containing vaping products have been linked to most cases of vaping-related illness. While vaping may be safer than smoking, we don't yet know for sure, and may not know for many years. For more information, check out the website of the US Surgeon General's office: e-cigarettes.surgeongeneral.gov.

Drugs and the Legal System

Most drugs are illegal to buy, use, and sell, including prescription drugs that are not prescribed for you. In the United States, all drugs are illegal if you are underage, including tobacco and marijuana. According to FBI statistics, there were 663,367 marijuana arrests in the United States in 2018. Almost 92 percent of those arrests were for possession. Of the 681,000 arrests of teens ages 18 and under for a variety of crimes, about 78,000 arrests were for drugs alone. Selling or dealing drugs carries much harsher penalties, often including jail time, than just having drugs in your possession does. However, if you are caught with a large amount of drugs, you can be charged with possession with intent to distribute, since it is assumed that you intend to sell drugs if you have a large quantity.

Since most drugs are illegal to buy, use, or sell, you risk getting yourself involved in the legal system if you choose to use drugs.

INEQUALITY IN DRUG ARRESTS

Drug arrests do not affect all groups equally. Even though rates of drug use are similar among various racial and ethnic groups, Latinos and African Americans are more likely to be arrested and more likely to face harsher penalties. Racial bias in law enforcement and the legal system in the United States greatly contribute to this disparity. People with lower incomes tend to live in places with higher crime rates, so police are more likely to monitor those locations too, making it easier to for them to make arrests. Teens from wealthier families can afford to hire attorneys to defend them and arrange for lesser penalties. While you may qualify for a court-appointed attorney if you can't afford a private one, you should know that many of these attorneys spend very little time on their cases. They might not even meet you until the morning of your court hearing.

If you are convicted, you may be placed on probation or even detained in a juvenile detention center. If you are on probation, you may have a curfew, be required to take drug tests, be ordered to participate in community service, or more. If you have a driver's license, it can be suspended so you can no longer drive. In some states, you can be tried as an adult for drug crimes, meaning that the consequences are much more severe. In general, the older you are, the greater the chances are that you will be charged as an adult if you are caught using or possessing drugs.

Once you have been convicted of a drug crime, you will have a record. This can prevent you from being hired for many jobs. In some cases, you may be able to petition the court to have your juvenile record destroyed.

You may also be disqualified from receiving federal student aid money for college if you have been convicted of a drug offense. When you complete the college financial aid form (the FAFSA), you'll be asked if you've been convicted of a drug offense. If you answer yes, you'll have to complete a worksheet to see if your conviction affects your eligibility for federal student aid. If your eligibility for federal student aid has been suspended due to a drug conviction, you may be able to get your eligibility reinstated by completing a drug treatment program.*

Legalization of Marijuana

Many states in the United States are pursuing the legalization of marijuana. Some states are legalizing it for medical uses only, such as to make you less nauseous while getting treatment for cancer or to help relieve chronic pain. Marijuana can also help people gain weight when they are losing too much weight due to an illness such as HIV/AIDS. In most states, you have to be 21 years old to use medical marijuana. Some states allow 18-year-olds to apply for medical marijuana if approved by a physician. Registered caregivers (such as parents) must approve applications for minors.

Other states are legalizing marijuana for recreational use. No states are legalizing it for recreational use for people under 18 years old, however. Some countries, such as Canada, allow citizens ages 18 and up to purchase marijuana for recreational purposes. One reason some people support legalization is that they believe that putting people in jail for possessing marijuana is a waste of time and resources. In the United States, some states have decriminalized possession of marijuana, meaning that the penalties for crimes related to

MEDICAL MARIJUANA

Some states have legalized medical marijuana for adults. A medical marijuana prescription involves joining a registry to get an ID card and having a medical evaluation. If a person has a qualifying diagnosis, they may be prescribed medical marijuana, which can come in many different forms including tablets, oils, patches, creams, and edibles. Smoking marijuana is often avoided in medical use because any and all smoke (even eating large quantities of smoked foods) increases the risk of cancer.

An advantage to medical marijuana is quality control. Patients get a high-quality product, customized for their needs–a lot different from buying marijuana off the streets, where you can never be exactly sure what you are getting.

---

* For more information about how a conviction might affect your eligibility for financial aid, see studentaid.gov/understand-aid/eligibility/requirements/criminal-convictions.

marijuana are less severe, so people are less likely to serve jail time or be charged with a felony.

But even if a state legalizes marijuana, marijuana is still against federal law in the United States, which means you can still get in trouble for possessing it. It is considered a Schedule I drug, meaning that it has no accepted medical uses, although this is slowly changing. This Schedule I status makes it harder to conduct good research on the effects of marijuana use.

You may think that just because a drug is legal for adults to use means that it is also safe. But just as with nicotine and alcohol, there are many risks associated with using marijuana. Marijuana use can lead to addiction, increase your risk of traffic accidents, damage your lungs, and impair your memory.

Other Concerns About Drug Use

Bringing drugs to school can result in loss of privileges (such as being able to participate in sports or extracurriculars), suspension, expulsion, or other disciplinary action. Your school may also get local law enforcement involved.

If you are pregnant, using drugs can affect your baby. Babies whose mothers use drugs can be born premature and underweight. Drugs can interfere with a child's intelligence and can cause a child to experience numerous behavior and learning problems later in life. If your baby is born with illegal drugs in their system, you may be reported to child protective services (CPS). CPS may take your baby from you and place them with another family member or a foster family. In some cases, your baby may be given up for adoption.

Your drug use affects other people and your relationships with them too. Some people justify using drugs because they think no one else is being harmed. This is not true. If you are using drugs, the people who care about you are probably worried about what might happen to you—you are adding to their stress. They might lose trust in you if you often lie about where you are and who you're with. Friends might not want to hang around with you if you are using drugs or if drugs change your attitude and behavior. If one of your parents has a security clearance for work, they could lose their job if you are arrested for possessing or selling drugs. If you become disabled as a result of drug use, your parents or guardians may have to care for you for the rest of your life.

Many teens in the United States die from drug use each year. The National Institute on Drug Abuse for Teens website reports that in 2018, 4,633 people ages 15–24 overdosed on drugs and died. If you are taking medications that are prescribed for you, such as Vyvanse, Adderall, or Concerta for ADHD, or Prozac (fluoxetine), Lexapro (escitalopram), or Zoloft (sertraline) for anxiety or depression, taking other drugs in addition to these medications can cause serious problems. Your medications may not work as well or may cause serious side effects if you take them while also using illegal drugs.

Drug use continues to be an issue for many teens, as well as many adults. Since illegal drugs come from many sources without any government oversight or enforcement of manufacturing standards, using them is especially risky. While some teens do not seem to experience negative effects, the risk remains high. Taking a more cautious approach is especially important when it comes to illegal drugs. If you think your drug use or someone else's is a problem, chapters 6 and 7 share ways to help you overcome your addiction and prevent relapse. For more information on teens and drug use, check out teens.drugabuse.gov.

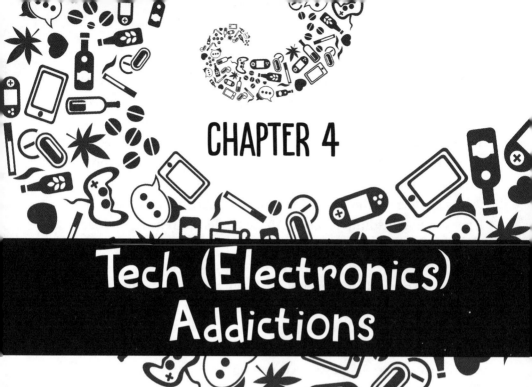

CHAPTER 4

Tech (Electronics) Addictions

"I've been depressed for a while and I'm not good at making friends. But playing *World of Warcraft* with people from all over the world helps me forget about my problems and stay connected. The problem is that I'm up all night playing, and then I can't get up for classes in the morning."

• • • •

"I wanted to be the best gamer of all my friends. I'd argue with my parents about my gaming, and I'd get really angry if anything got in the way of it. I spent all my money on gaming extras. My parents started limiting my play. My friends felt like I was ignoring them for my new gaming friends. But if I wasn't online when my gaming friends expected me to be, we wouldn't win our battles. I was the best one of my gaming friends."

• • • •

"I really like checking out my friends' posts on social media. Instagram and Snapchat are my favorites. I spend a lot of time checking my phone to see who has posted and how many people have liked my pictures and posts. It really bugs me if I don't get enough likes. Sometimes, I check my phone in the middle of the night because I don't want to miss anything, even though I promised my parents I wouldn't do that."

We use lots of electronic devices for school, communication, staying in touch with family and friends, art, entertainment, business, and learning about the world in general. Phones, gaming systems, tablets, and smart TVs are just a few. People can spend hours playing online games, watching funny videos, posting pictures on social media, chatting with friends, or streaming shows and movies. So what's the harm in that? Well, overusing electronics can cause big problems in your life, with family, school, friends, and even your mood. In this chapter, you'll learn about possible problems with electronics use and ways you can limit your use.

Use of Electronic Devices

According to the 2019 Common Sense media census, teens in the United States spend about nine hours a day on media devices, including reading on devices. Preteens spend about six. That's a lot of time! And adults spend their share of time on screens as well, whether it's for work or just posting cute pictures and funny cat videos online. At least half of all teens say that while doing homework, they often or sometimes watch TV, go on social media, text, or listen to music.

Many people think that "multitasking"—doing two or more things at once—doesn't affect their ability to complete tasks. However, what seems like multitasking is actually switching back and forth between activities. As a result, the quality of your studying may not be as good as you think if you are also checking social media and texting a friend. Although some people seem to be able to get important things done while messing around with their electronics, for most, this switching between tasks is distracting and disruptive.

Of course, everyone is unique, and some teens may be able to balance various tech activities and still accomplish what they need to do. As you read the next sections about gaming, phone, and social media addictions, try to take an honest look at yourself and your relationships to these devices and activities.

Gaming Addiction

Lots of kids (and many adults) enjoy playing video games. With the cool graphics and realistic characters, you can enter a whole new world, go on exciting missions, team up with others, defeat enemies, and totally forget about the world around you. If you are a gamer, chances are adults have to hassle you to get off the game and take care of your school and home responsibilities at least some of the time.

In the United States, 183 million people play video games on their consoles, computers, smartphones, or tablets. This includes 99 percent of boys under 18 and 94 percent of girls under 18. Across the planet, people spend **3 billion** hours a week playing video games. According to the *2019 Common Sense Census*, while gaming is the favorite activity of most boys, listening to music is the favorite for girls.

While most teens can stick to reasonable limits, some find that they prefer the virtual world of gaming to the real one. You may enjoy the control you have over your online characters, without the hassles of dealing with the actual people in your life and the problems that can arise. If you struggle with anxiety or depression, gaming can act as an escape from those feelings, which is partly why it can be so addictive. About one in 10 gamers becomes addicted to gaming.

For some people, gaming can activate the same brain areas that are activated when using drugs or alcohol. While gaming can improve your attention and reaction times, it can also change the structure of your brain, affecting your motivation and influencing what you find rewarding. Having a gaming console in your bedroom increases your risk for developing a gaming addiction. That's something to think about as you beg to game in private.

Another concern about excessive gaming relates to an increase in aggression. Some of the most popular video games are first-person shooter games and games that are otherwise aggressive in nature.

Most people don't become violent in real life after playing aggressive or first-person shooter video games; however, many of the teens who were involved in school shootings were obsessed with games like these. A study led by Dutch researchers found that teenage boys who pathologically game (have a gaming addiction) are more likely to become aggressive than those who don't.

Many gamers dream of getting rich by gaming. True, some earn big bucks, getting sponsors and streaming their gaming activities online. Being a YouTuber or livestreaming on Twitch might seem like a fun way to earn a living. But only around 3 percent of all YouTubers get about 90 percent of all views. Considering that getting views is how you make money, these are not very good odds. So if you're thinking you'll strike it rich by gaming, it's best to have a backup plan in mind.

While it has not been proven that these games cause violence, it is something to think about when you are evaluating your own gaming behavior. Pay attention to how you feel after playing violent or aggressive games. Do you feel calmer? Or do you feel more revved up, especially if you did poorly or were beaten by your opponents? Are you more likely to overreact with anger after gaming? If you're not sure, ask your family members what they think.

If video games increase feelings of frustration, anger, and aggression, why do people keep playing? Partly because video games are designed to be addictive. They are challenging, but not so challenging that you want to quit. You might often feel like success is just within reach, which leaves you wanting to play more. Another clever way that video game designers make their games more addictive is by using loot boxes. Downloading the game might be free, but you can buy better weapons or customize your characters if you have money to spend. The amount you spend may be small at first, but some kids and teens have stolen money to make these purchases. If you are using a family member's account on an app store, you may not even realize how much money you're spending until your family member gets the bill. Some gamers have spent thousands of dollars on their game addictions. Getting caught up in these types of gaming add-ons and in-app purchases can make you more likely to develop a gambling addiction.

The World Health Organization (WHO) now recognizes gaming disorder as a disease. Although some video game companies aren't happy about this, probably because they think it will affect their ability to make money, the recognition means that more money will become available for studying gaming disorder and how to treat it. It also makes it easier for people to get treatment for a gaming disorder or pay for treatment with medical insurance.

Signs You Might Be Addicted to Video Games

Although not all mental health professionals agree that gaming is a true addiction, there is no denying that it can cause big problems for some teens and their families. Here are some of the signs that suggest you might have a problem with gaming. See if one or more of these symptoms affect you or someone you know:

- repeatedly playing video games (including multiplayer online games) to the extent that your gaming causes significant problems in your daily life, such as not getting enough sleep, neglecting your homework, or even not caring about your hygiene or about keeping yourself well-groomed

- being obsessed with gaming to the extent that you spend much of your time thinking about gaming instead of other things you would usually be interested in
- feeling bad (depressed, angry, or anxious) when you're not playing video games
- wanting to spend more and more time gaming
- not being able to stop playing, even after you try to limit yourself
- losing interest in other fun activities, such as sports, hobbies, and going out with friends
- lying to family members or others about how much time you spend gaming
- using gaming as a way to feel less anxious, depressed, overwhelmed, or stressed—as an escape
- feeling that you would rather game than get involved in friendships or relationships

Maybe you recognize yourself in some of these symptoms, or maybe you recognize someone you know. People from all over the world can have problems with gaming. For example, China, with a population of over 1 billion people, has more online gamers—368 million—than the United States has people. Parents and mental health professionals in China describe *wǎng yǐn*, or internet addiction, as a mental health disorder. It is thought to affect about 24 million young people in China.

Kids and teens with ADHD are often more likely to have problems with gaming addiction. It's hard to pay attention to things that seem boring if you have ADHD. But because video games are constantly stimulating and changing, they can keep your attention for hours. This can make paying attention in class harder, since schoolwork may be a lot less interesting than games.

Also, if you have problems with depression or anxiety, gaming is more likely to become a problem since it can serve as a way to escape from those feelings. The dopamine boost you get from gaming can make you feel better, at least for a while. But after you stop, feelings of depression and anxiety can return, sometimes worse than they were before you started playing. This can drive your desire to play even more.

Phone Addiction

Many teens in the United States own a cell phone. A phone can be your connection to friends and family and to the rest of the world. However, many teens take their phones everywhere, including to the bathroom and to bed. According to a 2019 study by Common Sense Media, 39 percent of teens report feeling addicted to their phones. (And 45 percent of parents report that they feel addicted to their phones as well, so it's not just teens!) Sixty-one percent of parents think their teen is addicted to phones, while 38 percent of teens think their parents are addicted. Frequent phone users are more likely to be anxious, depressed, or aggressive and to have trouble paying attention.

If you have a phone, here are some signs you might be addicted to it:

- You feel a need to respond immediately to any messages you get.

- You constantly check your phone even when it doesn't ring or vibrate.

- You feel anxious or depressed when you can't use your phone.

- You ignore what is going on around you to focus on your phone.

- Your phone use causes arguments with family members and even some friends.

- If adults take your phone as a punishment, you go to great lengths to take it back.

- Your grades drop because you spend more time on your phone than doing your homework or studying.

- Your neck starts hurting because you are bending your head to look at your phone.

- You text or otherwise use your phone while you are driving, even though you know it's illegal, dangerous, and increases your chances of having an accident.

One of the first steps you can take to gain control over your phone use is to set times when you turn it off, put it in another room or in your bag or a drawer, or turn off notifications. Family mealtimes or other family activities should definitely be some of those times. Talking to family should be more important than responding immediately to a notification. Besides, checking your phone and responding to a text or notification in the middle of a conversation is rude. It can give the message that the person on your phone is more important than the person in front of you. Of course, if it's a parent or guardian contacting you, that's different. They probably expect you to answer when they call or text, or they might be contacting you for something urgent.

Try not to be on your phone or other electronic devices right before bedtime. The blue light that these devices emit lowers your brain's release of melatonin, a hormone that helps you fall asleep. Experts say you should put down your phone and other devices about an hour before you go to bed. That might not sound easy, but it's worth giving it a try. You'll sleep better and be less grouchy when you have to get up early for school.

If you use your phone as an alarm clock, turn off your notifications at night so you won't be awakened by them. And try putting your phone on the other side of your room when you go to bed. Not only will you not be tempted to use it in the middle of the night, you'll have to jump out of bed to turn it off in the morning, making it at least a little easier to wake up.

NEVER TEXT AND DRIVE

You've probably heard this many times. But what you may not know is that texting while driving, or even just holding your phone and talking to someone while driving, increases your chances of having an accident. In fact, texting while driving makes you anywhere from 2.8 to 23.2 times more likely to get in an accident. Texting makes you as dangerous on the road as if you were driving drunk.

Many phones can be programmed to send an automatic message to people who text you when you're in the car telling them that you're driving. There are also free apps available that can help you avoid texting and driving. Some, such as Drivemode, read text messages you receive out loud while you are driving. However, before you download an app, please stop and think. Even an app that reads incoming texts out loud can be distracting, especially if the message is upsetting.

To your own self be true! If there are days when having the radio on is too distracting or you find people talking to you while you drive disruptive, you know it's okay to silence them. So why not your phone? If you absolutely must respond to a text when driving, pull over when it's safe.

Social Media Addiction

Lots of people enjoy using social media on their phones or computers. It's a great way to stay in touch with people, find out what friends and acquaintances are up to, and let them know you follow them. It's fun to see who likes your posts, pictures, or videos.

But some people use these platforms excessively. Fear of missing out can keep people checking their devices frequently during the day, even when they're supposed to be in school listening to lectures or getting classwork done. (Have you ever had a teacher call you out for checking social media during class? If not, you likely know people who have!) Others use social media more than they actually talk with friends. Research suggests that the same areas of the brain that are activated when thinking about things such as money or sex are activated when you look at a picture and see all the likes you are getting. This is what can make social media so addictive.

Some people post very personal information on social media without realizing that others may see it. With Instagram, for example, you may have your rinsta account and your finsta account. On your rinsta, you post photos for a wider audience, while you keep more private thoughts, feelings, and pictures that you don't want everyone to see on your finsta. But you have to take care about where you are posting. It can be very embarrassing if you post to the wrong account by accident. Just because something is private doesn't mean it can't be shared without your knowledge or permission. Screenshots are easy for others to take and can cause you a lot of trouble if you share things you don't want the world to see or know.

Another problem with social media can occur when you see that your friends got together to have fun, but you weren't invited. This, among other reasons, is why social media use is linked to depression for many teens. Of course, you can't expect to be invited to every get-together. But it still hurts when you feel you've been excluded. You might feel like you weren't important enough to be asked.

⚡ TIP!
Think Before You Post
Many employers (and colleges) check applicants' social media accounts, especially if these accounts are public instead of private. If a potential employer sees pictures of you smoking weed, drinking, or talking about illegal activities, they may choose not to hire you. So if you are looking for a job, check your social media accounts first and delete any inappropriate posts. But remember, once something is online, there is no guarantee that it will disappear completely if you delete it. Even if you have a job, if your employer sees posts like this, you might lose your job. It's better to think before posting in the first place.

If you are a frequent user of social media, some signs that can indicate you have a problem include spending hours on social media, preferring to spend time on social media rather than hang out with friends, or feeling lost if you aren't on social media. You might also spend more time on social media than interacting with the people in front of you, even when you're hanging out with friends. This can make it hard for you to develop the social skills needed to form and maintain successful friendships. Think about this the next time you're with other people and are tempted to check your social media accounts.

Cyberbullying

A darker side of using electronics is cyberbullying. The website StopBullying.gov defines cyberbullying as bullying that occurs using digital devices such as phones, computers, or tablets to send, share, or post mean things about others that may be hurtful, embarrassing, or humiliating, whether or not they are true. Examples of cyberbullying include posting embarrassing pictures or videos; making fun of someone because of their gender identity, race, ethnicity, religion, or sexual orientation; spreading false rumors; and pretending to be someone else.

Using apps or the internet to embarrass or make fun of others is easy to do, and may seem funny at the time, but the harm you can cause is great. Even something intended as a joke may be taken seriously. Teens have committed suicide after being bullied or made fun of online. Some people who cyberbully go so far as to tell someone to commit suicide.

Apps can be especially harmful. For example, the Fess app allows you to post anonymously to your high school. The "anonymous" part makes it much more likely that cyberbullying will occur because people can say mean things without being identified or getting caught. The Down app looks through your Facebook contacts, and if two people find each other attractive, it helps them hook up. If no one finds you attractive, others might make fun of you for it. Blendr is an online dating app that lets you message, exchange photos and videos, and rate the hotness of other users based on the users' GPS locations. If your self-esteem is based on what others think of you, you may be devastated if you're rated as unattractive by peers. Most dating and meetup apps are for users who are over 18 years old. Pretending you are over 18 when using these apps can put you at risk since sexual predators also use them. If people who are over 18 meet up with you when you are underage, they could get in serious trouble as well.

RESPONDING TO CYBERBULLYING

If you find that you have been the target of cyberbullying, tell a friend or an adult you can trust. They can help you decide how best to handle it.

If you're in crisis and need someone to talk to, you can text the Crisis Textline at 741741 in the United States and Canada. Or call the National Suicide Prevention Lifeline at 1-800-273-8255.

Other Problems Associated with Electronics Addictions

A major problem with excessive electronics use is that you give up important things because of your use. You might skip meals, for example, leading to malnutrition. You might be up so late that you are not getting enough sleep—a serious problem since not getting enough sleep can lead to a host of other health issues. It can even shorten your life. Your relationships with family members and friends may suffer if you prefer interacting with your devices over the real people in your life. In addition, electronics use often encourages you to be sedentary. Not getting enough exercise can make you more irritable, cause you to gain weight, and make it harder for you to fall asleep. These are just a few examples of how excessive electronics use can affect you.

I'M NOT ADDICTED—I CAN STOP ANY TIME I WANT

See if you can go 24 hours without gaming, checking your phone, chatting online, or going on other social media. This is a great way to tell if you are addicted to electronic devices. Pay attention to how you feel. Was it pretty easy, or did you feel awful, as if something important were missing or you were completely disconnected from the world? Were you irritable, anxious, or depressed? What did you do with the extra free time you had? Even if you're not willing to give up your devices completely, you might decide to give yourself regular breaks from them.

Recovering from Electronics Addictions

"I didn't think I was addicted at first. But once I saw my grades dropping and my parents got on me about that, I realized that as hard as it was to admit, gaming was more important than anything else in my life."

• • • •

Recovering from electronics addictions is especially challenging. While you probably won't have any physical withdrawal symptoms, you would have a difficult time in today's world giving up electronics completely. You likely need a phone to be able to contact caregivers, stay in touch with friends, and use in emergency situations. More and more schools are using tablets and laptops as teaching tools, and you probably need internet access to get your homework done or check your grades.

So while you might never be able to give up electronics completely, if your electronics use has gotten out of control, there are things you can do to cut back. You may be able to set limits for your screen time in your phone's settings. You can also download apps that let you set limits for how much time you spend on your phone. Some options are Freedom, In Moment, Space, App Detox, and Off the Grid. Many of these apps charge money for their services, so check carefully. Zen Time is a free app you can use.

In addition, more treatment centers are now available for people with gaming and internet addictions. Rise Gaming Recovery in California is one such place. ReSTART in Washington state treats internet and gaming addictions and also provides useful resources as well as videos of people recovering from addiction on their website. Visit netaddictionrecovery.com. The Tech Addiction treatment center in Canada is another good resource. Their website techaddiction.ca contains useful information on recovering from electronics addictions. Gamequitters.com offers an at-home program for purchase (Respawn) to help people with gaming addiction.

You can also ask your parents or guardians for help if you can't control your electronics use on your own. There are many apps and internet tools that they can use to help. These include Net Nanny, Norton Family Premier, Kaspersky Safe Kids, Qustodio, OurPact, ESET Parental Control for Android, and MMGuardian.

Electronics addiction is a problem for people of all ages. We all use digital devices and it's hard to imagine how life would be without them. Still, the potential for addiction is a real concern. Even if you don't think your use of tech is causing severe problems, paying attention to how you use it may help you stay in control of your tech use, instead of it controlling you. For ideas on ways to feel good without using tech, see the sidebar on page 17.

CHAPTER 5

Other Activity Addictions

Kai likes going through pictures of hot girls on Tinder, looking to see if he can hook up. He does it so much that now he has a reputation as a player, making it harder for girls he'd like to date to take him seriously.

Milan likes exercising. It helps them keep their weight down and makes them feel good. But it seems like whatever Milan does isn't good enough. Now, they go to the gym for hours a day and restrict what they eat to make sure they don't gain weight. Milan says they're not hungry, but Milan's friends have noticed how thin they have become.

Jordan gets so anxious she can't stand it. Sometimes, she cuts herself with a razor. Seeing the blood makes her feel better, so she keeps doing it, but hides it by wearing long sleeve shirts, even in the summer.

Do these teens have a problem? This chapter will address other activities that can become addictive, including food, sexual activity, porn, shopping, self-injury, and gambling.

Addiction or Bad Habit?

Most activities are not addictive in the same way that drugs, alcohol, and technology are. Exercise and eating, for example, are normal human activities—we all have to do some amount of moving around and make sure we eat enough to stay alive. Sexual activity is also part of life as you get older. But for some, their relationships with these activities look a lot like addiction. Other activity addictions include shopping and gambling or betting. Self-injury (for example, cutting yourself) doesn't sound like an addiction, but for some people, doing it makes them want to do it more, even if it leaves scars that are embarrassing.

Some mental health experts think we shouldn't use the term *addiction* to describe having problems with these kinds of activities They don't cause physical dependence, and stopping them doesn't cause withdrawal symptoms in the same way that stopping drugs and alcohol does. However, experience (and recent research) tells us that activity addictions cause problems for many people. They can affect the same brain chemicals that are involved in using drugs.

Like electronics addictions, activity addictions can cause problems if these activities start interfering with other parts of your life. And the same strategies that help with drug, alcohol, and electronics addictions (see chapters 6 and 7) can help people manage unhealthy relationships to various activities. In this chapter, you'll learn more about these activity addictions.

Food Addiction

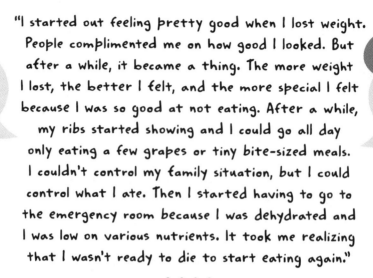

"I started out feeling pretty good when I lost weight.
People complimented me on how good I looked. But
after a while, it became a thing. The more weight
I lost, the better I felt, and the more special I felt
because I was so good at not eating. After a while,
my ribs started showing and I could go all day
only eating a few grapes or tiny bite-sized meals.
I couldn't control my family situation, but I could
control what I ate. Then I started having to go to
the emergency room because I was dehydrated and
I was low on various nutrients. It took me realizing
that I wasn't ready to die to start eating again."

• • • •

Many people struggle with food intake and making healthy
choices. Society puts a lot of pressure on people to be thin, and
people who are overweight are often teased, making it hard for
them to feel good about themselves. For some people, eating
certain foods activates the same pleasure centers of the brain
that are activated when using drugs or alcohol. And it's not just
overeating that's a problem. Eating too little, trying to starve
yourself, or purging after you've eaten can also become addictive,
as well as dangerous. These behaviors can eventually lead to an
eating disorder such as anorexia or bulimia.

Foods with fat, sugar, or salt are especially addictive. The
advertising slogan for Lays potato chips used to be, "You can't eat
just one." Makers of these foods know what to put in them to make
them hard to put down. Salt, sugar, and fat are especially tasty and
can ramp up your appetite for more. You've probably eaten more
than you intended on some occasions. Maybe the chocolate cake at
someone's party was so good you couldn't have just one slice. Or
you open a bag of tortilla chips planning to have a few, and next

thing you know, you're in front of the TV having eaten the whole bag! Most of us might binge eat once in a while, and other than feeling uncomfortably full, it doesn't cause problems.

But people with a food addiction have serious problems limiting what they eat. They keep eating even though they know it is causing issues. Some people go on eating binges where they eat an entire day's worth of food at one time, even if it makes them sick to their stomachs later. It's as if they don't have an off switch for their appetite. Having a food addiction doesn't mean you are overweight, but many people who are addicted to food can become overweight because of their addiction. Being overweight increases your risk for developing many health-related diseases, such as heart problems, high cholesterol, and diabetes. If you develop diabetes, you may eventually need to give yourself insulin injections to control your blood sugar levels if your pancreas becomes damaged by poor blood sugar control.

See if you can relate to some of these signs you may have a food addiction:

- eating more than you had planned or feeling an irresistible urge to overeat
- experiencing intense guilt and shame over how much you ate
- continuing to eat even after you don't feel hungry anymore
- thinking a lot about food
- spending a lot of time getting food, preparing it, and eating it
- eating so much that you feel sick
- repeatedly trying to reduce your eating or starving yourself to be so thin that your bones stick out
- avoiding certain situations, such as parties or restaurants, because you're afraid you'll overeat or are embarrassed when others watch you eat
- overeating to avoid feeling anxious or self-soothing with comfort foods

Food addictions and overeating can cause health problems over time, and some eating issues can become severe enough for someone to be diagnosed with an eating disorder, which is more dangerous and may lead to death if not treated. Eating disorders include anorexia nervosa, bulimia nervosa, and binge eating disorder.* Anorexia occurs when someone feels overweight even when they are not and will starve themselves to be thinner. People with anorexia often eat very few types of food and will count each calorie to make sure they don't gain weight.

With bulimia, people will eat a large quantity of food in a short period of time, more than most people eat. They can't control themselves when doing it and afterward, they feel bad and will make themselves vomit or take laxatives to avoid gaining weight. If this pattern happens at least once a week for three months, a person will meet the criteria for a diagnosis of bulimia nervosa.

People with binge eating disorder go on eating binges to the point that they feel sick. They eat very fast, can't control how much they eat, and often feel ashamed or guilty afterward. But with binge eating, people don't make themselves vomit or take laxatives. People with binge eating disorder may occasionally vomit spontaneously as the body tries to cope with an overload of food.

Eating disorders are dangerous because of what they do to your body. When you starve yourself, your body starts taking nutrients out of your muscles. Since your heart is a muscle, your risk of having a heart attack increases. Young people with anorexia between the ages of 15 and 24 are 10 times more likely to die than others their age. If you vomit repeatedly, you can damage your esophagus and rot your teeth. Taking laxatives can make you dehydrated, which can be life-threatening as well. Repeated use of laxatives and vomiting changes your blood chemistry, making you prone to seizures even if you've never had them before.

---

* In this book, anorexia and bulimia are shortened ways to refer to anorexia nervosa and bulimia nervosa, respectively, which both represent a group of symptoms. In a medical description, the word anorexia alone can refer to a loss of appetite, while the word bulimia is a term for overeating.

Most people with eating disorders need therapy. Sometimes medications can help. In severe cases, you may need to be hospitalized. The National Eating Disorders Association (NEDA) has many resources for you to explore if you think you may have an eating disorder. They also have an online test you can take to help you self-diagnose. For more information, check out their website nationaleatingdisorders.org. You can also call their helpline during the week at 1-800-931-2237. If you are in a crisis, you can send a text to their crisis line; text "NEDA" to 741741 to be connected with a trained volunteer.

There are also self-help groups for people with eating issues, such as Food Addicts Anonymous (foodaddictsanonymous.org). Overeaters Anonymous is a 12-step program for people with problems related to food, including, but not limited to, compulsive overeaters and those with binge eating disorder, anorexia, and bulimia. Visit their website oa.org for more information. Food Addicts in Recovery Anonymous (foodaddicts.org) is another self-help program.

HELP FOR EATING DISORDERS

If you are struggling with symptoms of anorexia, bulimia, or binge eating, seek medical attention. These disorders can cause serious physical problems.

Sex and Love Addictions

Some people become addicted to sexual activity, including using dating or hookup apps. While most dating apps say you need to be 18 years old to use them or that you need parental permission if you are under 18, the reality is that most teens don't bother to ask permission. If you are LGBTQ+, you might be more inclined to use apps for dating or hookups if you fear that approaching potential partners in person could result in harm to you. While a dating app may seem innocent enough, sexual predators also use these apps to find victims. Be sure never to meet someone privately who you have communicated with only through the app. People often aren't who they say they are. Some popular dating and meetup apps for young people include Yubo, Bumble, Taffy, Skout, Happn, and Coffee Meets Bagel, although most of these apps are for users who are 18 or older.

Other apps, such as Tinder and Grindr, make it easier than ever to find people who want to hook up and have sex. While some people use dating apps because they want to find someone to date, others use them to hook up with people they don't know. This behavior can become addictive when it seems like you're always looking to hook up and that doing so just makes you want to keep doing it, even when it causes problems.

Rates of sexually transmitted diseases (STDs) have risen recently, making hooking up risky. While some STDs can be cured with antibiotics, others, such as herpes and HIV, stay with you for life, though taking antiviral and other medicines can help with both and using condoms can help protect your sexual partners from getting these diseases. If you've experienced trauma in your life, such as being physically or sexually abused, you are at greater risk for developing a sex addiction. Initiating sexual activity after you've been abused can feel like a way of taking your power back from an abuser. It is important to be honest with yourself about the quality of your relationships if they seem to be only about having sex.

Some people feel better about themselves when they can brag about the many people with whom they've had sex. But this can leave you, as well as the partners you've left behind, feeling empty and lonely. Girls are often judged negatively when they have a reputation for sleeping around, while boys may be proud of their behavior, though these distinctions are not true for all people. Think about the reputation you want to have when deciding how you want to approach others and how you want others to perceive you. Nobody likes to be used or to be seen as a user.

Some sexual addictions may actually be a love addiction. The title of the self-help support group Sex and Love Addicts

Anonymous reflects the fact that these addictions often go together. For example, some people use sex as a way of getting or feeling love. You might think that by agreeing to have sex with someone, your sexual partner will fall in love with you, making you feel better emotionally. However, this often isn't the case, and it just leaves you feeling more sad, lonely, and depressed.

People with a love addiction are often terrified of being alone and will do anything to keep a relationship from ending. If you have a love addiction, you might be attracted to people who "need fixing." You think that if you succeed in helping your partner, you will have earned their love and they will stay with you forever. You may also focus only on making your partner happy, ignoring what you want or need. This usually fails, since people who are needy often have trouble maintaining healthy relationships. For more information about sex and love addictions, check out the Sex and Love Addicts Anonymous website slaafws.org.

> **TIP!**
>
> **Let's Wait Awhile**
> One way of telling if someone is interested in dating you is to hold off on any sexual activity until you get to know the person. Some say that the "best" sex organ is the brain, meaning that sex has a deeper connection when two people really get the way each other thinks and know what each other likes. People who just want to hook up won't wait around. But someone who is interested in you as a person will. It's a good test.

Porn Addiction

Addiction to pornography is another form of sexual addiction. Viewing online porn is common among teens. According to a survey by the University of New Hampshire, 93 percent of boys and 62 percent of girls have viewed porn during their teenage years, and 64 percent of teens and young adults view porn on a weekly basis. It may seem like such activity is harmless—after all, who is hurt if the behavior only involves you?

In fact, such behavior can cause multiple problems. Viewing porn, particularly videos, can give you a false idea of what people actually like to do sexually in real life. It can make you feel inadequate if you compare yourself to people in videos. Many porn stars have breast implants or larger than average sex organs. Who can compete with that?

Viewing porn, especially lots of different images and videos, can make you crave variety, making it difficult to be interested in actual people your age. You may look forward to watching it so much that you'd rather do that instead of other activities you used to enjoy.

More extreme porn, particularly when it involves violence, force, or even underage people can give the impression that those actions are okay in real life. But it's against the law to share sexual pictures or videos of someone who is underage, including yourself. And it is never okay to use violence or force to get someone to have sex. Finally, many people in the porn industry, especially women, are taken advantage of by the people who make the porn.

While it may be true that you are not hurting anyone (or engaging in risky behavior that can result in pregnancy or an STD) by watching porn, think about how it may be affecting what you think about sex. Porn addiction can cause problems in relationships, often because men may be more interested in viewing porn than in being intimate with their partners. It's a lot easier to masturbate to porn, only thinking about yourself, than it is to seek out relationships and get to know people first. The dopamine rush you get from masturbation can make intimate contact with others feel boring in comparison, causing problems in your relationships as you get older.

Some people who watch porn compulsively and masturbate while watching it become desensitized to sexual activity. Over time, watching porn can get old and you may need to do it more often or seek out more extreme pictures and videos, which can make you think that what you see online is normal. If you view porn that features people under 18, you can get in trouble with the law too, even if you are underage yourself.

Finally, you may be putting yourself at risk by seeking out online porn. You may be asked to meet someone you don't know to engage in sexual activity. You may be offered money for sending nude pictures or recording yourself performing sexual acts. If you give into this, the other person can use that information to pressure you to send more pictures or videos, or they may threaten you in some way, such as sharing your private pictures with others. This is illegal. Should this happen, let an adult you trust know. Never give your personal information, such as your real name, address, or phone number online. Just as your browsing history can be monitored by internet trolls, your viewing habits can also be monitored by those who may be looking to exploit you.

If you watch porn, monitor how often you do it. Avoid anything that is aggressive or violent and avoid clicking on pop-ups you haven't requested. If you think you have a problem with porn, try not looking at it for a period of time and see what happens. If you can't go a week without it, you may have a problem.

Sexting Addiction

Sexting is another potential form of addiction. Many teens have participated in sexting, which involves sending or receiving explicit sexual messages and pictures over text. Some people sext because they see having these pictures and messages as a kind of trophy, giving them bragging rights with friends. Others might feel attractive when someone asks for their picture. If you're in a relationship, you may feel pressured to send such messages to your significant other, not realizing that the person can share these images with their friends, especially if you decide you want to break up later. This is not only humiliating and a form of bullying but is also illegal in many states. In 2009, Cincinnati teenager Jesse Logan committed suicide after a nude photo she had sent to a boyfriend was circulated around her high school, resulting in harassment from her classmates.

Sexting, when it involves underage teens, can get you arrested for distributing child pornography. Even if you are underage yourself, having nude pictures of anyone under 18 on your phone or computer is illegal and is considered child pornography. Being labeled as a sex offender as a teen has serious consequences that can stay with you for a long time. This can happen even if you are the one sharing pictures of yourself! Always remember that once pictures or videos of you are on the internet, they can be impossible to remove.

The website That's Not Cool (thatsnotcool.com) was created to help teens with problems related to digital dating, including pressure to text too often or send pictures you're not comfortable sending.

Self-Injury Addiction

Self-injury is when someone intentionally hurts themselves by cutting, scratching, burning, or other forms of damaging behavior. Studies show that about 17 percent of teens have self-injured at least once. Most teens who self-injure aren't trying to kill themselves—a common misconception. Instead, self-injuring can be a way for people to keep from killing themselves because it relieves painful emotions. In a way, it's like the person is distracting themselves from emotional pain by replacing it with physical pain that they control. Teens who self-injure are also more likely to use drugs or alcohol, and many have other addictions.

Most people don't think of self-injury or self-harm as an addiction. However, it does have an addictive quality. For example, if you feel better after self-injuring, at least temporarily, you might be tempted to do it more and more often, especially when you feel upset. As with other addictive behaviors, self-injury can trigger a release of endorphins that make you feel better—less depressed, less anxious, and less angry. It's this release of endorphins that makes this behavior addictive. You may find it hard to resist the urge to keep hurting yourself, which is a similar feeling to when people addicted to drugs resist the cravings to keep using.

Self-injury is also risky, since it increases the chances that you may cause yourself more serious harm. If you cut too deeply, you could hit a vein or artery. Scars can last a lifetime and can communicate to others that you are a cutter. People who self-injure are more likely to make suicide attempts. And some activity fads, such as choking to the point of unconsciousness to feel high or make sex better, can tragically and unintentionally lead to death.

One type of treatment that can help people who self-injure is called DBT—dialectical behavior therapy (see page 117). DBT teaches people how to manage their emotions in healthy ways. With DBT you can learn to tolerate and regulate unpleasant emotions such as anxiety, improve your ability to get along with others, and be more mindful in your dealings with yourself and others.

SAFE (Self-Abuse Finally Ends) Alternatives is an excellent resource for teens and adults who self-injure: helpguide.org /articles/anxiety/cutting-and-self-harm.htm. Some people find it helps to rub ice on their arms or snap themselves with rubber bands as safer substitutes to self-injury. Squeezing stress balls, journaling, or writing on yourself are other safe ideas that leave no scars.

Helplines are available as well when you are feeling the urge to hurt yourself. In the United States you can call SAFE Alternatives at 1-800-366-8288. Canada also has a kids' helpline you can call for any issue, including injuring yourself: 1-800-668-6868. In the United Kingdom, you can call the Mind Infoline at 0300 123 3393 or text 86463.

SELF-INJURY

If you are concerned that your self-injury might lead to attempting suicide, tell someone immediately. You can also call the National Suicide Prevention Lifeline in the United States at 1-800-273-8255.

Shopping Addiction

Many teens enjoy shopping. Getting new clothes, a new video game, or a new phone can be exciting. Even the act of shopping and trying to get the best deal is a fun challenge for some. But for other people, the enjoyment they get is on a whole other level. It can feel compulsive when the urge to shop and buy stuff gets in the way of other activities. As with other addictions, the release of endorphins and dopamine feels so good that you want to feel that way all the time.

Signs of a shopping addiction include:

- spending hours shopping or buying
- shopping to make yourself feel better when you're anxious or sad
- not being satisfied with what you already have
- spending more money than you have on buying stuff
- stealing money from others, including from your parents or siblings, so you can buy things
- arguing with parents or guardians over things you want to buy

Most teens don't have many financial responsibilities, so shopping usually doesn't cause serious problems. You also don't have a lot of money to spend. But if this behavior lasts into your adult years, it can cause more serious problems. If you spend so much money that you don't have enough to pay your rent, your student loans, or your car insurance, you can get in serious trouble. Many adults struggle with credit card debt, which can keep people from being able to rent an apartment or buy a car. Sadly, giving in to the urge to buy only makes you feel better for a while. Shopaholics find that they need that rush of buying so badly that they can't even truly enjoy the items they purchase. The urge to shop can also be associated with bipolar disorder.

Gambling and Betting Addiction

Betting on games, sports, or cards is a fun activity for many people. The idea of winning a lot of money is exciting. If you enjoy gambling or betting, never bet more than you can afford, and don't overreact when you lose, then it may not be a problem for you. However, for others, gambling or betting quickly becomes an addiction. They can't control their impulse to gamble, and this gets them in trouble. For example, adults who have a gambling problem may bet their rent money on a game or a race that they are convinced will turn out how they expect it to. When they lose, they can't pay rent, which can lead to many issues. If you spend money you can't afford to spend on gambling or betting, you probably have a problem with it.

According to the website YouthGambling.com, while over 60 percent of teens report gambling for money, only about 4 to 5 percent of kids ages 12 to 17 have one or more symptoms of a gambling problem. While most teens only gamble once in a while and just for fun, some develop serious problems. Boys are more likely than girls to gamble and experience gambling problems. Betting on sports games is one of the most common types of gambling, but playing cards or even buying lottery tickets can also lead to a gambling problem.

In many states, the minimum age for gambling in a casino is 18. For people of any age, the best way to approach visiting a casino is to decide how much you are willing to lose and to take only that amount in *cash* (do not bring credit cards, debit cards, or checks). If you go gambling with friends, tell them not to let you borrow from them. That way, if you end your trip to the casino with more money than you brought, you've beaten the odds. If you spent all your cash but enjoyed the buffet and the time with your friends, the evening was still worthwhile, and you didn't overspend.

Signs that you might have a gambling problem include selling your stuff to get money to gamble, owing people money for gambling debts, sneaking family members' credit cards or stealing to get money to gamble, and spending hours at online gambling sites.

People with a gambling problem are often convinced that if they just keep playing, they will eventually win big, or at least win back the money they lost. Some websites encourage this by promising you a chance to win something big if you buy chances or tickets. Loot boxes in video games are similar: you spend money to get better tools to use in the game, only to find out that they aren't as good as you thought. You buy into it, betting that you'll get something really good, only to be disappointed.

For more information on gambling and betting addictions, check out the website teenhelp.com/money/teen-gambling. Gamblers Anonymous (gamblersanonymous.org/ga) is another resource for help.

Activity addictions share many characteristics with drug, alcohol, and electronics addictions. If you feel better afterward, it's understandable why you'd want to keep doing them. But it's important to remember that all addictions can hurt you and that learning to deal with unpleasant emotions without resorting to addictive behaviors will help you a lot more as you get older. Chapters 6 and 7 share more information on how to do this.

CHAPTER 6

Getting Help With Addictions

"Kids always brag about winning on Fortnite. My parents keep an eye on my use, and I have to earn it. But whenever they are out of the house, I look in their bedroom to take my controllers back. My parents stopped trusting me because of it. I didn't think they had the right to control my use until I realized that the game was controlling me. It took my parents taking the Xbox out of the house before I realized it was a problem."

• • • •

Having an addiction can seem overwhelming. You may have tried repeatedly to cut back on your use, only to go back to using again. The rate of relapse (going back to using after a period of not using) is pretty high. Still, there are many things you can do to manage your addiction.

Recovery from addictions is hard work! You have to break old habits, such as turning to drugs, alcohol, or other addictive behaviors to deal with life's problems, and replace them with new, healthier habits and behaviors. In this chapter, you'll learn about the recovery process and various treatment strategies to help you overcome your addiction. All the strategies can help with substance use addictions, and many can help with activity addictions. It is important to find the ones that work for you.

The Stages of Recovery

"I've always known my drinking could become a problem. But I figured I could keep it under control if I just tried harder. I could stop for a while, but then I'd go back to getting drunk. Now my parents have threatened to take away my driver's license. I want to reduce my drinking, but I'm not sure I really want to give it up."

• • • •

"I was scared to go to a support group meeting because I thought it would be a bunch of old guys talking about how bad their lives are. But I wasn't getting better on my own. After I decided to give it a try, it was a lot better than I expected. There were a couple of guys close to my age and a lot of people gave me their numbers in case I felt like drinking again. After going, I felt a lot more hopeful that I could beat this."

• • • •

"After I decided to put my phone down during parts of the day, especially at dinner and when I'm with family, I don't feel like I have to check it all the time. It actually feels freeing. We started a game night at home, and I know I wouldn't enjoy it as much if I were glued to my phone. I've told my friends I might not respond right away so they don't think I'm ignoring them."

If you're not ready to give up your addictive behaviors yet, that's okay! Being ready to make such a big change often occurs in stages. A few decades ago, researchers James Prochaska, Carlo DiClemente, and John Norcross came up with a theory of stages of change. Their theory was based on what they observed in people who decided to change their problem behaviors. The six stages they outlined are as follows:*

Stage 1: Precontemplation. This is where most people start. During precontemplation, you're not even thinking of making a change, since you don't yet see your behavior as a problem. Perhaps you haven't had many (or any) negative consequences as a result of your behavior. You think you're fine.

Stage 2: Contemplation. In the contemplation stage, you're willing to consider the possibility that you have a problem but have mixed feelings about whether you need to deal with it yet. You're willing to learn more about addiction and weigh the pros and cons of your behavior as well as the pros and cons of making a change.

Stage 3: Preparation (Determination). At this stage, you're ready to make the change and are willing to take the steps needed. You realize you have a problem. You may come up with a plan for how you'll make the changes needed to overcome your addiction. You might decide to quit completely, use less, or just take a break from using and see what happens. Getting rid of your triggers (things that make you want to use) is often part of the preparation. If you smoke cigarettes, for example, you might prepare by throwing away your remaining cigarettes and lighters. If you are quitting weed, you might throw away all paraphernalia, such as bongs and rolling papers. If you're stopping addictive eating, you might get rid of high-calorie snacks. One of the toughest parts of this step is thinking about your friendships and relationships. For example, if most of the people you hang out with use weed, you may have to distance yourself from them so you're not tempted to use. Or you

---

* For more information about the stages of recovery, visit psychcentral.com.

might avoid going to your friends' houses while they're gaming if you are trying to cut back or stop your own gaming activity.

Stage 4: Action. This is when you follow through with your plan. Often this means telling other people of your decision to stop your addictive behavior. Letting people know you are trying to stop can make sticking with it easier. If people catch you drinking, smoking, or playing video games, for example, after you made your commitment to stop those activities, they can talk with you about it. It also makes it harder for you to go back on your commitment if others know about it. For teens, it can help you figure out who your real friends are, since friends who want to see you succeed are less likely to tempt you to go back to your addictive behaviors. If your problem is severe enough, you might start the action stage with treatment, such as counseling, hospitalization, or residential treatment.

Stage 5: Maintenance. After you have stopped your addictive behavior, the challenge now is to maintain your recovery. Relapse can happen, but your goal is to get back on track as quickly as you can if you do relapse, to minimize any harm that might occur as a result. This stage can take months. For activities you can't give up completely, such as eating, spending, or going on the internet, you may decide on limits and work on sticking to them. For example, if you are a binge eater or overeat on a regular basis, you might count your calories or use a calorie tracker to monitor your food intake. If checking social media is your addiction, you might try limiting your use to an hour a day, using a timer to help keep yourself in line. You'll learn more about maintenance in chapter 7.

Stage 6: Termination. At this point, the temptation to relapse is much lower and staying sober or free of addictive behavior becomes easier.

The stages of recovery are a good guide to help you understand the steps you may need to take to overcome your addictive behaviors. Not everyone goes through each stage at the same pace.

You might take longer in one stage before being ready to move on to the next. You don't need to rush—focus instead on what works best for you.

Deciding If You Are Ready to Quit

Often, people who are thinking about stopping an addictive behavior have mixed feelings. Part of you might want to keep your addiction going because it's fun or relieves unpleasant feelings, while another part of you thinks that maybe you should stop. Motivational interviewing is a therapy technique used by counselors to help people decide whether they are ready to quit. Here are some questions you can ask yourself when making your decision:

- What are some of the good things about your addiction?
- What are some of the not-so-good things about your addiction?
- What makes you think you might need to make a change?
- What do you think will happen if you decide not to change?
- How would your life be better or worse if you decide to quit?
- Why are people in your life concerned about your behavior?
- If you decide to change, how confident are you that you can do it?
- What's the best thing that could happen if you quit?
- What's the worst thing that could happen if you decide not to quit?

Try writing your answers to these questions in a journal, computer, or your phone, then read them aloud. Sometimes, hearing yourself say it helps you see yourself more clearly.

You can also make a chart comparing the pros and cons of continuing to use and quitting. If you are trying to quit using drugs or alcohol, your chart might look something like this.

	Pros	Cons
Making a change (quitting)	I'd be in less trouble. I would do better in school. My parents would trust me. I would be healthier.	I'd have to stop going to parties. I wouldn't have as much fun. I might have to change my friends.
Not making a change (not quitting)	I'd still have fun. I'd keep hanging out with friends. It would be easier to keep using.	I'd be in more trouble. My parents will ground me. I might have to go to residential treatment. I might get arrested.

The Recovery Process

Recovering from an addiction isn't easy. Up to 40 percent of alcoholics who are in counseling and alcohol support groups will relapse despite their best efforts. People with drug and other addictions have similar trouble reducing or stopping their use. It can help to view a relapse as a sign that you need to make more changes in your life or adjust your recovery plan. You'll learn more about strategies for dealing with relapse in chapter 7. Don't lose hope and don't give up. Quitting your addiction gets easier if you keep at it. It will get better!

Early recovery can be difficult, depending on how addicted you were. Your body may react to losing its favorite way to deal with problems or have fun. Your brain creates cravings to get you to start again. Don't be fooled—this is normal and will pass if you give it time.

Withdrawal

If you stop your addictive behavior suddenly, you may experience symptoms of withdrawal. Your brain and body will react when you first stop using alcohol or drugs, and you may have some or all of these withdrawal symptoms: tiredness, vivid dreams, sleep problems, muscle twitches, skin problems, aches and pains, cravings, memory loss, mood swings, and trouble performing sexually. These are all normal and generally pass. The longer you used and the more frequently you used, the more likely you are to experience at least some of these symptoms. This is particularly true if your drug of choice was alcohol or an opiate such as heroin or OxyContin.

Some people experience post-acute withdrawal syndrome (PAWS) after stopping their use of alcohol. Alcoholics may start having PAWS symptoms about two weeks after they stop using. Symptoms can include trouble thinking clearly, memory problems, emotional overreactions or numbness, sleep problems, physical coordination problems, and oversensitivity to stress. In some cases, PAWS symptoms can last for 6 to 12 months. These symptoms reflect the brain's attempts to repair the damage caused by alcohol or drugs. You need to give your brain time to heal so it can function normally again without drugs or alcohol.

While withdrawal symptoms are most noticeable with drug and alcohol addictions, some people experience symptoms (usually anxiety, irritability, anger, and depression) when trying to stop other addictive behaviors. For example, if you are quitting gaming or social media, you'll probably feel more anxious and irritable when you stop. You might even have more trouble sleeping.

If you experience any symptoms of withdrawal, be sure to talk with a doctor. They can help you manage it and can sometimes prescribe medications to help you get through the worst. If you aren't seeing a doctor for your addiction, talk to an adult you trust, such as a parent or guardian, school counselor, or teacher. They will be able to help you find medical assistance or research support groups and other treatment options. Next are common withdrawal symptoms for alcohol and other drugs.

Alcohol: anxiety, trouble sleeping, irritability, fever, sweating, headaches, upset stomach, trouble thinking, seizures (In severe cases, people can suffer from delirium tremens, or d.t.'s, which can cause you to experience severe confusion, shake, hear voices or see things that aren't there, think others are out to get you, and have increased blood pressure and heart rate. This is rare for teens but can occur in adults after years of heavy drinking.)

Depressants (Xanax, Valium, Klonopin): sleep disturbances, restlessness, irritability, anxiety, panic attacks, tremors, sweating, seizures, hallucinations, nausea

Stimulants (cocaine, crystal meth, ecstasy, nicotine, Ritalin, Adderall): anxiety, tiredness, irritability, trouble concentrating, stomachaches, diarrhea, hunger, depression

Narcotics (heroin, Vicodin, OxyContin): sweating, restlessness, irritability, stomachaches, diarrhea, tremors, sneezing, loss of appetite, cramps, trouble sleeping

Psychedelics (marijuana, LSD, ketamine, mushrooms): agitation, trouble sleeping, anxiety, irritability, confusion, sweating (These symptoms are more common with marijuana, which is used more frequently, than with drugs such as LSD or mushrooms, which are used less frequently.)

Types of Treatment

Some people can stop using alcohol or drugs or engaging in addictive activities pretty easily. Once they decide to stop, they don't go back. They may not need treatment if stopping is this easy for them. It may be that their symptoms of addiction were less severe. But for most people, it's hard to stop doing something that you've enjoyed and that has helped you in some way, even when you know it's not good for you.

Many treatment options are available to help people overcome addictions. Some people do better with one than with another, while others may need more than one type of treatment.

Most insurance plans now cover the cost of treatment for alcohol and drug addictions. Treatment for other addictions that are not recognized as disorders is generally not covered unless you have another mental health disorder such as ADHD, anxiety, or depression. Usually, you'll have to pay for a portion of the treatment, even with insurance. If you don't have insurance, most cities and counties in the United States have public mental health and substance abuse centers that are free or low cost. You can search online to find a center in your area. Some schools also provide free counseling. If not, your school counselor or another trusted adult might have some information on places you can go for help. Self-help and support groups for addictions are a free option. See the list of support groups in the resources section for contact information.

As you read the next sections about the various kinds of treatment, try to keep an open mind. Being open to treatment and being willing try it if you haven't, or to try a new kind of treatment, might help you recover faster.

Counseling/Therapy

When trying to beat an addiction, most people start with individual or family outpatient counseling. In this kind of counseling, you meet with a therapist or counselor, usually once a week, to figure out what might be driving your addictive behavior and come up with ways that can help you stop, or at least control, your behavior to the point that it doesn't cause problems. Counseling can last for a few weeks or many years, depending on how helpful you think it is and how hard it is for you to improve. It is important to have a counselor who understands addictions, since not all are trained in this area.

CONFIDENTIALITY CONSIDERATIONS

Confidentiality in counseling means that counselors or therapists keep what you say to them private. This makes it easier for you to share your feelings, thoughts, and behaviors, some of which you may feel embarrassed about and wouldn't want anyone to know. However, there are limits for what counselors can keep private. If you talk about feeling suicidal, a counselor may have to tell your parents or guardians to help you stay safe. Sharing about your addictions can be tricky. If you are doing dangerous things, such as drinking and driving, your counselor will need to tell your parents or guardians because these behaviors could kill you or others. Other activities that are not dangerous, such as sneaking your phone back in the middle of the night, may be things your counselor can keep private. Be sure to ask your counselor how confidentiality works and what things they cannot keep private.

Family therapy is an important part of treatment for teens. Chances are that you and your caregivers have had a lot of conflict over your addictive behavior—such as yelling, punishments that seemed too harsh, and fighting about lying or stealing. Adults often don't know how to handle teen addiction, and their fear of something bad happening to you may come out as anger instead of concern. Or maybe they don't want to believe you have a problem. Family therapy can help teens and their caregivers talk about these issues and figure out ways of working together that help everyone.

Some therapists have teens and adults make a written contract about expectations during recovery. This contract might include items such as curfews, the consequences for using, and privileges you will gain as you make progress. Doing this can cut down on disagreements, since everyone has to follow the contract, including adults.

Some people may also have group counseling as part of their treatment. Group counseling involves meeting with a therapist and other people with addictions. Some groups are more educational, and the counselor teaches you about addiction and suggests ways to address it. Others are more process groups—this means that you talk about addiction as well as other things that may be a part of the problem. Some teens find it easier to talk in a group counseling setting where other teens are with them, while others may feel more comfortable talking one-on-one with a counselor.

Medication

Psychiatric medications can help some people stop addictive behavior. If depression is driving your addictive behavior, for example, taking medication to treat your depression can make it easier to stop using. Some medications, such as Narcan, can help reduce cravings for drugs. Suboxone is used to help people addicted to narcotics such as heroin, codeine, and OxyContin. Not only does suboxone reduce cravings, it keeps other narcotic drugs from working if you do take them. Other medications include Vivitrol, Antabuse (disulfiram), Topamax (topiramate), Zyban or Wellbutrin (bupropion), Chantix, Nicoderm, Nicotrol, and Nicorette gum. More medications are being tested every day. Psychiatrists, nurse practitioners, and even some family doctors and pediatricians may prescribe these medications. Ask your counselor if you have questions about using medication as part of your treatment and whether it would be helpful for you.

Intensive Outpatient Therapy

Intensive outpatient therapy (IOP) is one step up from individual or family counseling. You'll go for therapy two or three times a week, usually for a few hours at a time. Most IOP programs focus on group counseling. Talking to other teens who have problems with addiction can help you feel less alone. You can get support from others your age and learn what they do that helps them. You might be able to help the others in your counseling group as well, which feels good and can help you stop using. If you are in school, you will have to work hard to complete your school assignments so you don't fall behind when much of your time is spent in IOP.

Inpatient Treatment/Hospitalization

Inpatient treatment (hospitalization) can help when you are unable to make progress using individual, family, and group counseling or medication. In a hospital, you won't be able to use drugs or alcohol or engage in other addictive behaviors. This type of treatment can also help if you are having suicidal thoughts and it's not safe for you to get treatment while living at home. If you are addicted to alcohol or narcotic drugs (such as heroin or OxyContin), it is often safer to stop using in a hospital setting to make sure you don't have problems withdrawing. For example, it can be dangerous for people who drink heavily every day to just stop using because it can cause a seizure. In a hospital, you can be given medication to keep this from happening. People usually stay in the hospital for a few days or weeks, depending on how long doctors and counselors think you need to be there. If you are in school, you will need to work on your school assignments to the best of your ability while you are hospitalized.

Residential Treatment

Residential treatment is the most intensive type of therapy. It usually lasts more than 30 days (and can last up to six months or more) and is a long-term hospitalization, though it doesn't take place in a hospital. Caron Treatment Centers in Pennsylvania and Florida are well-known centers for treating teens. If you and your parents or guardians decide that you need this level of treatment, you will need to find out how much it would cost, since these programs are very expensive. If you have health insurance, you will need to check to see what centers your insurance will approve.

Some treatment centers understand that you might continue to use drugs while you are in treatment and will work with you, while others may decide to discharge you from their program if you test positive for drugs or alcohol. Be sure you understand the rules before you start a program.

While most residential programs are for people with addictions to drugs or alcohol, there are a number of treatment programs now for people with internet or video game addictions. Some popular programs include American Addiction Centers, Newport Academy, and Outback Treatment. Summer camps for gaming addiction include Camp Pocono Trails, Reset Summer Camp, and Summerland Camps, to name a few. Trails Momentum in North Carolina offers treatment for teens with tech addictions. Be sure to research these places with your parents or guardians to see if they are covered by insurance and to make sure that they would be a good fit for you and that they have a good reputation.

Boot Camps

These centers use a military-style training model to help teens recover from addiction or delinquent behavior. They teach discipline, involve physical training similar to a military boot camp, provide simple meals, and expect teens in the program to help with cleaning and other tasks. Strict obedience to rules and schedules is required.

While this method may be helpful for some teens, for others it can also cause worse problems. These centers are often not regulated and some of the staff can be abusive. In some countries, such as China, these centers are used for people addicted to the internet. If you have problems with depression or anxiety, boot camps may not be a great option. If your parents or guardians are considering sending you to a boot camp, ask them to research various camps to see if they are licensed, how costly they are, and if any complaints have been reported about them.

Getting help for addictions can be scary, especially if you have never been in counseling before. But giving it a chance to work can make the difference in recovering from an addiction.

Support Groups and Self-Help Groups

Support groups can be a great way to meet other people who are trying to recover from addictions. Even if you're not sure you're ready to quit, listening to other people's stories about how addiction has affected their lives can be eye-opening. Going to support group meetings can be part of your treatment plan as you recover, or it may be something you continue after you have finished your treatment to help you avoid relapse. Also, support groups are free! If there aren't any groups where you live, you can find many online support groups that might be able to help. See the resources on page 145 for a list of support groups.

12-Step Support Groups

Twelve-step support groups for addictions have been around for a long time, and they are free. Alcoholics Anonymous (AA) is one of the oldest self-help groups for addictions. Meetings are safe places where people can connect with others in recovery or still trying to get sober or clean. While most groups are for adults, there are some teen groups. Similar support groups exist for people who use other drugs, such as Narcotics Anonymous (NA), Cocaine Anonymous, Heroin Anonymous, and Marijuana Anonymous. The 12-step program is used to help people with other addictions as well. Examples include Food Addicts Anonymous, Food Addicts in Recovery Anonymous, Gamblers Anonymous, Nicotine Anonymous, Overeaters Anonymous, Sexaholics Anonymous, and Sex and Love Addicts Anonymous.

These groups are called 12-step programs because they outline 12 steps people should take when trying to overcome an addiction. These programs suggest focusing on "one day at a time," meaning you can choose not to use "just for today," instead of promising yourself you'll never use again. Admitting that you are powerless over your addiction is a central part of 12-step programs. You might decide not to use, but once you use, you are powerless to control it.

Some people have a problem with the concept of a higher power that is a central feature in AA, NA, and other 12-step programs. For many, their higher power refers to God or another supernatural being. But not everyone believes in a higher power, or the same higher power. You don't have to go along with this to get help using a 12-step program. Some people choose to think of their higher power as being the best version of themselves that they can imagine once they are free from their addiction. Also, the idea that you are "powerless" over your addictive behavior can feel like you have no control over your addiction, which may or may not be true.

AA, NA, and other 12-step groups have been around for a long time and have helped many people. One of their slogans is "Keep coming back. It works if you work it!" Other 12-step slogans include "Keep it simple," "Take what you need and leave the rest," and "Bring your body— your mind will follow." You may fight it at first, but there is something very healing about being around others who know what you're going through. They automatically get your struggle, which may not be true for friends or family who don't struggle with addiction.

People in 12-step groups often have a sponsor. This is someone who has been in recovery for a longer time and can help guide you through the program. You can contact your sponsor when you are

Is Alateen for You?

If you are struggling with an addiction, chances are that someone else in your family has similar problems. Alateen is a self-help group for teens who have parents or other family members who are addicted to alcohol or drugs. Groups meet in person or online and give teens a chance to share their concerns about a loved one's addiction and learn ways of supporting each other.

The people close to you can also get help for themselves if they are having a hard time handling your addiction. Families Anonymous is a support group that can help them. For more information, check out their website familiesanonymous.org.

feeling down or like using. A good sponsor who knows you well may be one of the first to spot warning signs of relapse (see page 112). Twelve-step programs recommend that you have a sponsor who is of the same gender if you are heterosexual or the opposite if you are gay or a lesbian. This may be different if you are bisexual, pansexual, aromantic, or asexual. The point is to avoid choosing a sponsor whom you might potentially have romantic or sexual feelings for, since that will interfere with your recovery. This is very important, because your sponsor is a kind of mentor, helping you achieve greater independence and self-reliance. You may even become someone's sponsor one day.

You should also try to find a home group, which is the meeting time and location you feel most comfortable attending. As a teenager, you'll want to pick a meeting with other teens if possible. Each group has its own vibe, so you may have to shop around until you find the group that's right for you.

You can start attending meetings at any point in your recovery. The only requirement is that you want to stop your addictive behavior. Some people at the meetings will be new to recovery, while others have been

MAKING AMENDS

Twelve-step programs include making amends as part of your treatment. This means thinking about all the people you may have hurt while drinking, using drugs, or engaging in other addictive behaviors. Apologizing to everyone you've hurt can be very tough emotionally. This is why these programs recommend waiting to do this until later in recovery. Steps 8 and 9 address this challenge. If making amends feels too hard for you right now, wait until you have been in recovery for a while before taking this step. When done at the right time, taking responsibility for your past actions, asking for forgiveness, and, sometimes, being forgiven can be liberating and empowering.

Another way you can make amends is to volunteer or do things for others. Help clean up in your neighborhood; offer to help your parents, friends, or siblings; visit someone who is lonely; or reach out to someone at school who sits alone. These actions can make you feel better about yourself, which helps in your recovery.

in recovery for years. All members work through the steps at their own pace. Check online to find meetings in your area. Visit aa.org for AA meetings and na.org for NA meetings.

SMART Recovery Self-Help

SMART Recovery (SMART stands for Self-Management and Recovery Training) is an alternative to 12-step groups designed to help people help each other with addiction. SMART Recovery uses a four-point program. The first point involves helping people develop and maintain the motivation to change. The second focuses on ways to cope with urges to use or engage in addictive behavior. In the third, participants learn to manage their thoughts, feelings, and behaviors effectively without slipping back into addictive behaviors. Finally, participants learn how to live a balanced, positive, and healthy life.

SMART Recovery does not use labels such as "alcoholic" or "addict," but they do focus on being abstinent. For more information on SMART Recovery, check out their website smartrecovery.org.

Rational Recovery

Rational Recovery is another alternative to 12-step groups. They are known for their Addictive Voice Recognition Technique (AVRT). They call the voice of addiction "The Beast" and teach that it represents the part of you that tries to convince you to continue addictive behaviors. It tricks you by saying things such as, "Just do it once. You can control it!" or, "Life will be awful if you stop using." It will do anything to get you back to using.

By recognizing when your "Beast" is telling you to use, you can develop coping strategies to help you talk back to it and not listen to it. Telling your beast that you will never drink (or use drugs) again can be very helpful once you have made the decision to stop your addictive behavior. Try saying, "Hey, Beast—get the f*** away from me. No way am I going to let you run MY life." You can also give your addiction a name. Telling yourself that "Fred" is trying to trick you to go back to using can make it easier not to listen. Humor can help break the urge to use because you're using the thinking part of your brain. (See the explanation on page 124.) For more information on AVRT and Rational Recovery, check out their website rational.org.

Co-Occurring Mental Health Disorders

Many people who struggle with addictions also have other mental health disorders. Commonly co-occurring disorders include depression, anxiety, bipolar disorder, and ADHD. Often, people with these disorders turn to addictive behaviors in an attempt to feel better or self-medicate. People with mental health disorders are more than twice as likely to struggle with addictions.

While addictive behaviors may help you feel better for a while, that doesn't last as addiction sets in. Addictive behaviors usually make mental health problems worse. If you are to be successful in overcoming your addiction, it's very important to also get treatment for any co-occurring disorders you have. This may mean taking medication. For example, binge eating can raise levels of the neurotransmitter serotonin, which can become depleted if a person has problems with depression or anxiety. Therefore, taking medications that help raise serotonin levels can help people with a food addiction control the urge to overeat. However, since medications often interact with alcohol and other drugs, making them less effective or even dangerous, it is important that you tell your treating doctors about any substances you are using. They may be able to help you handle cravings by adjusting your medication or adding another one.

Some doctors and treatment programs will not prescribe medication for other mental health conditions if you are still actively using. It is risky to do so, since using drugs can interact with the medications you are being prescribed. Also, if you are just stopping drug or alcohol use, it is hard to tell if your symptoms are due to withdrawing or to mental health issues such as anxiety or depression. Still, sometimes treating your mental health disorder sooner rather than later can make it easier for you to quit using alcohol or drugs.

A Word of Caution, and Hope

You might think that once you make the decision to get help for your addiction, you'll never go back to it. Sadly, that's not necessarily true. Many people, perhaps as high as 70 to 80 percent of those who complete treatment programs, relapse. That's discouraging. But that doesn't mean you've failed. It means that your addiction was stronger than you thought, and it will take more effort to overcome it. If you have made progress before, you can do it again. And you can go even further. It may be that your brain has been so damaged by excessive alcohol or drug use that it can't absorb all the information you are getting while in treatment. It can take months for your brain to heal.

This is why it's important to take full advantage of whatever treatment programs you and your caregivers choose. These programs know how hard addictions are to beat, so do your best to listen to their advice. Many people want to leave treatment as soon as they start. But give it time. Ask hard questions if you disagree or don't understand what you are being taught. And keep at it, no matter how hard or how hopeless it seems. It gets better.

CHAPTER 7

Preventing Relapse

Relapse is when someone who had stopped abusing drugs or alcohol goes back to using them. With other addictive behaviors, a relapse is when someone resumes the behavior after a time of successfully avoiding it. Since relapse is common for people with addictions, it's important to think about it ahead of time and take actions to help avoid it. In this chapter, you'll learn more about relapse, ways to prevent it, and what to do if you relapse.

Relapse or Recurrence of Symptoms?

Not everyone likes using the word *relapse*. For example, if you are treated for cancer and your cancer comes back, you don't say you relapsed. Instead, it's a "recurrence of symptoms." Some people believe that using the word *relapse* implies that you are choosing to go back to abusing drugs or alcohol. While in a way it is a choice, the disease of addiction can take over and push you toward using, even when you know it's not a wise thing to do. It's like the addiction takes control of your body and your brain. If the word *relapse* feels hopeless to you or makes you feel like you've failed, you might try thinking about it as a recurrence of symptoms instead.

A *slip* (or a *lapse*) also refers to going back to addictive behaviors, but it is not as severe as relapse or recurrence. If you end up getting high with a friend, feel bad about it, and stop after that one instance, that is a slip. A relapse is when you continue going back to your addictive behavior. While a slip may be easier to deal with, you should still take it seriously, since slips can easily lead to a full-blown relapse. Don't beat yourself up about a slip, but try to figure out how it happened and what you need to do differently to avoid another one.

In recovery, you might feel like you have two different sides to yourself. Dr. Harold Urschel, author of the book *Healing the Addicted Brain*, talks about recovery as a battleground between pro-addiction and pro-recovery thoughts. The pro-addiction thoughts aren't very accurate, because you may not be thinking clearly when you first give up your addiction. Drugs and alcohol change the way your brain operates. Pro-addiction thoughts might sound something like, "I have more fun when I drink," "I can stop anytime I want," or "It's not a big deal—my parents should just get off my back." Learning to talk back to pro-addiction thoughts using pro-recovery thoughts can help you stay sober. Pro-recovery thoughts are thoughts that remind you why you gave up your addiction in the first place and the good things that come with being sober.

"My brother died of an overdose of heroin years ago. I've been mad at him ever since, and mad at myself for not realizing how bad he was getting. That helps me stay off drugs."

• • • •

"Weed really helped me go to sleep. But after I tripped on LSD, I started having hallucinations, especially at night. I knew they weren't real, but it still scared the crap out of me. Things coming at me and leaving. Now, whenever I get high, it happens again. Me and drugs don't mix."

Since the two main motivations behind any addictive activity are to deal with unpleasant emotions and to stir up excitement, one of the keys to preventing relapse is to improve your ability to handle your feelings and have fun without the use of drugs, alcohol, or other addictive activities. Read on to learn more about the relapse process and some excellent ways to prevent it. For more ideas on how you can feel good without using drugs or alcohol, see the sidebar on page 17.

The Relapse Process: Identifying Triggers and Warning Signs

Relapse is a process, not an event. This means that relapse begins long before you slip back into addictive behavior. It starts with little things, such as going to a party where you know there will be alcohol to see if you can resist the urge to drink or spending time around your drug-using friends to see if you are strong enough to say no while they're all getting high. Later, you may start telling little lies to family and friends about where you are and who you're with or thinking that you can control your use if you go back to it. Thinking, "One drink can't hurt. I promise it'll be just one!" while knowing that it is never just one drink for you can lead you down the wrong path. By identifying your triggers and checking for signs of relapse at least once a week, you can stop the slide into a full-blown relapse. Writing down these thoughts in a journal can help you keep track of them and figure out what works and what you might need to change.

To avoid relapse, you need to figure out your own personal triggers and warning signs so that when they occur, you can take action. Triggers for relapse are things that make you want to use again or go back to addictive behaviors. They can be people, places, events, items, activities, feelings, and bodily sensations. Warning signs include thoughts, feelings, or behaviors that indicate that you may be getting close to having a relapse.

Relapse Triggers

Triggers get their power from being connected in your brain to your addictive behavior. For example, if you are a gamer, every time you see a computer or controllers, your brain associates that image with the rush you get when you play. When your brain expects a rush from gaming, but you don't game, it remembers how good it felt to game and pushes you to want to do it again by making you crave it. Scientists call this classical conditioning. It's why your dog gets excited, jumping up and down, when you open the cupboard to get his food. He doesn't even see the food yet, or smell it, but he gets excited because he knows what's coming.

One way of remembering the more common triggers for relapse is to remind yourself to HALT. Ask yourself if you are **hungry**, **angry**, **lonely**, or **tired**. Proper eating, expressing anger appropriately, interacting with people in healthy ways, and getting plenty of rest are all excellent ways to stay sober and avoid slipping back into addictive behavior. Look at the following list of triggers and make a note of all the ones that apply to you:

- hanging out with drug- or alcohol-using friends
- having a bad day
- going to places where you used to use drugs or alcohol or engage in other addictive behaviors
- staying up too late or not getting enough sleep
- getting into arguments with family members or friends

- seeing things that you associate with your addiction (for example, bottles, rolling papers, cash, the number of your dealer popping up on your phone, or a friend showing you their latest social media posts)
- smelling smoke from a joint
- being home by yourself or feeling lonely
- getting notifications on your phone
- watching people play video games or seeing an ad for the latest version of your favorite game
- feeling overwhelmed; having too much you have to get done
- wanting to celebrate something good that happened
- getting paid so you have money you could spend on addictive substances or behaviors

What other relapse triggers can you think of? Keep your list in a journal, on your computer, or on your phone.

Warning Signs of Relapse

As you read earlier, relapse usually doesn't just happen. There are signs along the way that, if you learn how to read them, will warn you that you are getting dangerously close to a relapse. A combination of warning signs and triggers increases your risk for relapse. Most people find that the longer they wait to act, the harder it is to stop. It's like a snowball rolling downhill, getting larger and larger. If you act soon, you can stop it at the top of the hill, where it's still small and rolling slowly.

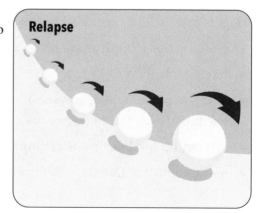

Relapse

But if you wait until it's so large and so fast that you can't stop it, relapse is going to happen—it's just a matter of when.

If you recognize any of the following warning signs of relapse in yourself (or in a friend you are trying to help), now is the time to take action. Be honest with yourself when reading these warning signs:

- wanting to discontinue counseling
- thinking about how fun it was to use drugs or alcohol or engage in other addictive behaviors
- feeling increased irritability—little things set you off
- being in denial—thinking that your problem wasn't really that bad
- being overly confident—thinking that you can control your use this time
- lying about where you are and who you're with
- using different drugs than the one you quit (for example, using marijuana after you quit drinking), thinking that they won't cause the same problems
- being impatient—thinking that you should have felt a lot better by now
- feeling bored—thinking being sober is boring and you need more excitement in your life

What other relapse warning signs can you think of? You can include your current warning signs and those you've had in the past. Add them to your list of relapse triggers in your journal.

Now that you know what your relapse triggers and warning signs are, you can come up with a plan for what you can do when they happen. The following ideas and strategies can help you lower your risk for relapse. Give them a try and see which ones work best for you.

In learning about the signs of addiction and relapse, you may recognize them in people you care about. Suggesting to someone that they might have a problem isn't easy, especially if they aren't ready to admit it themselves. Still, you may be in a position to help. Rather than telling someone that they are addicted and need help, try a gentler approach. For example, you might say something like this: "Hey, can I talk to you about something? Lately I've noticed that you seem to be drinking a lot, and I'm concerned about how it might be affecting you." If you have been in counseling yourself, you could share your experiences and suggest that the person might benefit from it too. Even if the person turns you down, you can still let them know that you're here for them if they ever want to talk. If you know that someone is doing dangerous things such as driving after drinking or using drugs to the point that they could overdose, talk to an adult you trust (such as parent, older sibling, or school counselor) to see if they can assist the person in getting help.

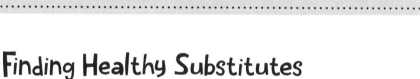

Finding Healthy Substitutes for Addictions

Since addictive behavior is often a way to relieve boredom, you'll need to find substitute activities to pursue if you want to succeed at conquering your addiction. This will also help fill up the free time you'll have by giving it up. Activities such as walking, running, going for a bike ride, playing sports, deep breathing, listening to music, watching movies or TV shows, taking a warm bath or shower, reading, watching a funny video, writing in a journal, or talking to a friend or family member are all healthy ways that people spend their free time and avoid boredom. Hobbies such as painting, drawing, doing crafts, playing an instrument, or writing music also help you pass the time and give you a sense of accomplishment. Chances are you wouldn't have enjoyed these activities as much while you were using, because addictive behavior ramps up your dopamine to such high levels that ordinary activities seem boring as a result.

You might also consider getting a part-time job or volunteering in your community to help others who need it. Joining a club at school can introduce you to new people. Other possibilities for combatting boredom include organizing a game night with friends, starting an exercise program (which is more fun if you have someone join you), playing street hockey or another sport, or building a fort in the woods.

Even helping your parents or guardians more around the house can help. Learning to cook is a life skill and offering to prepare a meal for your family, even just once a week, would be appreciated by them. This can also be a way of thanking your family for the things they have done for you. Showing gratitude helps you maintain a positive attitude, which helps in recovery.

THE DREAM OF CONTROLLED USE

Most people who give up an addictive behavior wish that they could go back and control their use, as they may have been able to do when they first started drinking, smoking weed, or gaming. This is understandable–who wouldn't want to think that they can go back to controlled use? However, thinking like this is a warning sign for relapse. While it may be true that some people can reduce their use to a manageable level, if your problem was bad enough that you needed treatment, you're not likely one of these people. You are *always* taking a risk if you attempt to go back to controlled use. And there's no guarantee that you'll survive another binge, especially when more dangerous drugs are involved.

Learning to Manage Your Emotions

Since many people end up with addictions as a way of avoiding unpleasant feelings, learning how to handle uncomfortable emotions in healthier ways is an essential part of any relapse plan. Challenging emotions, such as anger, worry, and sadness, are powerful triggers for relapse.

Anger is a powerful emotion. It is triggered when you feel hurt or threatened. Anger helps you stay safe when you need to fight or run away from actual threats. But those actions aren't so helpful when you're mad at someone for making fun of you, telling you that you can't do something, breaking up with you, or not giving you what you want.

Learning to change how you think about situations is an effective tool in managing emotions. Instead of taking everything personally (for example, "She did that on purpose just to make me mad!"), try to look at the situation from the other person's point of view. Maybe she had a bad day, or maybe she's upset with you for something else. Take some deep breaths and check out your assumptions to see if your thoughts are accurate. You can ask the person, "Were you trying to make me mad by saying (or doing) that?" You can also let the other person know how you're feeling. But take care to do this in a tactful way—that is, say it in a way the other person can hear. For example, telling someone, "You were a real jerk to me when we were at lunch today," is likely to get a defensive or angry response. Instead, try to use an I-message and stay calm. Here's one example: "I felt really upset when you made fun of me at lunch in front of everyone. Maybe you were trying to be funny, but it wasn't funny to me."

Anxiety, worry, and fear also increase your risk for relapse. They are unpleasant feelings and can cause headaches, stomachaches, a racing heart, and shallow breathing. Most people want those feelings to go away as fast as possible. If your go-to addictive activity worked well at relieving your anxiety, of course you'll think about it when you become anxious or worried, which can trigger cravings. Some people mistake anxiety for a craving. You might think that using is the only thing that will make your worried feelings go away. But anxiety doesn't last forever. Strategies such as deep breathing, talking back to anxious thoughts, going for a walk, or just talking about your feelings can all help lower your anxiety. Many people with past trauma find fulfillment in practicing yoga or meditation. Remember: *Anxiety does not last forever*, even if it *feels* like it might.

One method for learning to manage your feelings is to use skills taught in dialectical behavior therapy (DBT). According to DBT, many people in their daily thoughts think about bad things that happened in the past or worry about things that may happen in the future, instead of focusing on the present moment. With DBT, you can learn how to handle situations that cause you stress, regulate your emotions, improve your relationships with others, and solve problems effectively.

DBT talks about your emotional mind, your reasonable mind, and your wise mind. Your emotional mind is driven by feelings and instincts and doesn't think about consequences, while your reasonable mind operates on logic and reason alone and doesn't take how you feel into account. Your wise mind, or wise self, takes the best of both: you listen to what your feelings are telling you and you use logic and reason when deciding how to act. If you find you are thinking of using, try to look at the situation from your wise mind. Ask yourself if you are speaking from your emotional mind, your rational mind, or your wise mind. For example, you can say "My emotional mind is telling me that I can't handle my anxiety without using, but my wise mind tells me that going for a walk and waiting it out will work better if I give it a try."

DBT is based on another method of dealing with thoughts and emotions—cognitive behavioral therapy (CBT). CBT teaches that emotions such as sadness, anxiety, or anger are the result of distorted beliefs people hold about situations or events in their lives. Most people think that feelings just happen and that they have no control over them. However, it is often a thought that triggers a feeling, and a feeling that can trigger behaviors. This process, also called the ABC model, happens so quickly that you may not even realize that a thought started it.

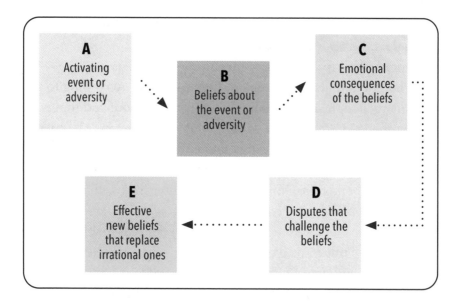

Developed by psychologist Albert Ellis, the ABC model explains the relationship between thoughts and feelings. In it, *A* stands for an **activating** event, *B* for the **beliefs** or thoughts you have about the event, and *C* for the emotional **consequences** of those thoughts. For example, if your significant other dumps you (the activating event), you will most likely feel sad. That's normal. If you believe or tell yourself that no one will ever want to date you and that you are a loser (your thoughts about the event), you will feel very sad, and perhaps angry, and are more prone to depression, as well as going back to addictive behavior to cope with the feeling (the emotional consequences of your thoughts). But if your belief about being dumped is that you are still a worthwhile person and that you will find someone else, you won't feel as sad.

There are two additional steps to this model that help you fight back. *D* stands for **disputing** (disagreeing with or talking back to) any of your thoughts, such as coming up with different ways to interpret the event. Using the example of being dumped, if you tell yourself that you're a nice person, that not everyone will be attracted to you, and that the right person just hasn't come along yet, you won't feel so depressed. If you do this, it will lead to *E*—a new **effect** that feels much better.*

Building Your Social Support System

People with addictions often have trouble in their relationships with others because the addiction takes the place of relationships. Establishing meaningful connections with other people can be very effective at filling the emptiness inside that often fuels addiction. It is true that relationships can be riskier if you have problems with addiction. Significant others might break up with you, and friends might unfriend you, which can be triggers for relapse. Even so, people with healthy friendships, relationships, and family connections are happier and feel less of a need to use addictions as a substitute.

Alcoholics Anonymous (see page 102) talks of avoiding "people, places, and things" in recovery. People you have used with before, places you have used before, and items that go along with using are all things to avoid, at least at first. Just as a dog knows that a person opening the cupboard where the dog food is stored means she's going to eat soon, your brain connects using with the people you've used with, the places you've used, and the things you needed to have for your

⚡ TIP!

Have a Code or Safe Word

If you are out with friends and they are using alcohol or drugs in ways that make you feel unsafe or that trigger you, you might hesitate to leave on your own because of what your friends might think. One way around this is to make a plan with your parents or guardians for an escape word or phrase. If you text your parents this word or phrase, they will call or text you saying that there's an emergency and that they will pick you up immediately. This lets you save face by giving you an out with your friends without feeling embarrassed. The adults also need to agree not to criticize or punish you for doing this, which keeps you safe and them less worried.

---

* The Positive Psychology website has a good article that explains this further: positivepsychology.com/albert-ellis-abc-model-rebt-cbt.

addictions, such as drug paraphernalia or your controllers or other gaming devices. So just seeing some of these people, places, or items can cause you to have cravings, which can lead to relapse.

Giving up friends you've used with is one of the hardest parts of recovery. After all, if you have a substance use problem and most of your friends are drug or alcohol users, or if you are trying to give up gaming but most of your friends are gamers, who are you going to hang out with? Expanding your group of friends so that you can hang with people who don't use drugs or drink alcohol, or who don't game, is important. This is why counselors frequently recommend that teens join 12-step groups. Meeting others your age who are also trying to recover from addiction can help you build new connections and support your recovery. Joining a club or sport can also help in making new friends. You can even think back to people you used to hang out with before you got into your addiction. Is there someone you used to enjoy spending time with? If you let that person know you've decided to quit, they might be more open to spending time with you again.

If an old friend from when you were using says they want to see you after you are in recovery, try this strategy suggested by Caron Treatment Centers. Agree to meet with your friend if the first time you meet is at one of your recovery groups. That way your friend can understand what your recovery is all about. This is a good way to separate the friends who really do support you from the ones who just want you to use with them again. You might be surprised at how many of your friends eventually end up in recovery themselves. Introducing a friend who uses to the recovery process is a way to make amends (see page 104) and another way to fight addictions.

Pursuing a Healthier Lifestyle

Most addictions involve activities that make you feel better, whether that means feeling less anxious or sad or feeling more energized and less bored. Part of the challenge of recovery is to find other healthier ways to handle these feelings. These replacements are sometimes called "positive addictions" because they make you feel better without the problems of your addictive behaviors, though they aren't really addictions.

Exercise is one of the most important substitutes for addictions. Exercise helps your brain release chemicals called endorphins, which can improve your mood and give you more energy. The trick is to find ways to make exercise more fun. Having someone with whom you can work out, go for walks, ride bikes, skateboard, or join organized sports helps a lot. Don't expect exercise to make you feel better right away. It takes time for it to become something you look forward to doing. Still, even just going outside to take a walk is good for your health in so many ways—from strengthening your immune system to increasing your blood flow and muscle mass and even to ensuring you get enough vitamin D.

Getting enough sleep is another healthy change you can make. Many teens have trouble getting enough sleep, often because they are up late doing homework, texting friends, posting on social media, gaming, or watching videos or TV. Over time, not getting enough sleep makes you feel tired and less focused. This can trigger the urge to pursue addictive behaviors. Coffee or energy drinks can make you feel better temporarily, but these can also be addictive since they contain the drug caffeine (see page 37). And ironically, they make it harder to fall asleep!

Eating a balanced diet is important as well. Getting plenty of fruits and vegetables, healthy proteins and fats (such as beans, nuts, or fish), and whole grains, and avoiding processed foods and sugary foods, can help your brain repair itself while it gets used to operating without the rush of addictive behaviors. For more information about what is included in a balanced diet, check out Harvard Medical School's Healthy Eating Plate (health .harvard.edu/healthy-eating-plate). This model was developed as a healthier version of the USDA's My Plate plan (choosemyplate .gov). These plans replace the Food Pyramid that was used previously. Other countries have their own graphics to help people make healthier eating choices.

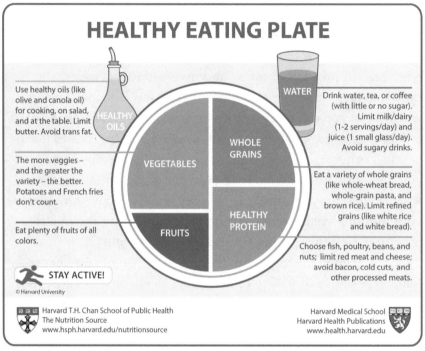

HEALTHY EATING PLATE

Use healthy oils (like olive and canola oil) for cooking, on salad, and at the table. Limit butter. Avoid trans fat.

HEALTHY OILS

The more veggies – and the greater the variety – the better. Potatoes and French fries don't count.

VEGETABLES

Eat plenty of fruits of all colors.

FRUITS

WHOLE GRAINS

HEALTHY PROTEIN

WATER

Drink water, tea, or coffee (with little or no sugar). Limit milk/dairy (1-2 servings/day) and juice (1 small glass/day). Avoid sugary drinks.

Eat a variety of whole grains (like whole-wheat bread, whole-grain pasta, and brown rice). Limit refined grains (like white rice and white bread).

Choose fish, poultry, beans, and nuts; limit red meat and cheese; avoid bacon, cold cuts, and other processed meats.

STAY ACTIVE!

© Harvard University

Harvard T.H. Chan School of Public Health
The Nutrition Source
www.hsph.harvard.edu/nutritionsource

Harvard Medical School
Harvard Health Publications
www.health.harvard.edu

Copyright © 2011 Harvard University. For more information about The Healthy Eating Plate, please see The Nutrition Source, Department of Nutrition, Harvard T.H. Chan School of Public Health, http://www.thenutritionsource.org and Harvard Health Publications, health.harvard.edu.

Developing a healthier lifestyle may not seem like it is related to recovering from addiction, at least not at first. But taking better care of your body with exercise, good sleep, and healthy eating also helps your brain work better. By making your health a priority, you may find that you have more motivation to stay healthy, including avoiding addictive substances and behaviors.

Other Coping Strategies for Preventing Relapse

"The hardest part of recovery for me was giving up my drug-using friends. But once I stopped, no one wanted to hang out with me anymore. I guess they weren't my real friends. I started reaching out to some of my old friends who don't use drugs and realized that I had missed them more than I expected."

• • • •

"I'm still tempted to sneak my phone at night to text my friends and post on Instagram. My parents finally started trusting me with my phone, and I don't want to lose that privilege. Also, my grades started improving and we've been getting along better at home too. After sneaking it one night, I put it back and decided life was easier sticking to my limits."

The more strategies you have that you can use when you are tempted to return to addictive behaviors, the more successful you will be. Once you find a strategy that works for you, write it down. You can carry a notecard with you or put a note in your phone so you can look at your strategies whenever you need to use them.

One of the challenges of recovery is that the cravings you might feel to go back to your addiction may actually be normal emotions bubbling up. If you were used to dealing with your feelings with your addictive behavior, normal human emotions may be unpleasant at first. It will take

> ⚡ **TIP!**
>
> ## Relapse Prevention Jeopardy!
>
> If you are working with others who are also trying to prevent relapse, try playing the online game Relapse Prevention Jeopardy! You can pick teams and answer questions related to relapse. For more information, check out their website playfactile.com/relapseprevention.

time for your brain to get used to them without wanting to go back to unhealthy ways of coping. Do your best to be patient—it doesn't happen overnight.

Here are some additional strategies that can help you manage urges to use or go back to addictive behavior. Think about how these might help you succeed in resisting those urges.

Addictive Voice Recognition Technique

Use the Addictive Voice Recognition Technique (AVRT) as described in the book *Rational Recovery*. Observe your thoughts and feelings about your addiction. Those thoughts and feelings that support continued addictive behavior are called your addictive voice. Picture this voice as coming from an "It," and not from you. Some call this voice their "Beast." Instead of thinking "I want a drink," say to yourself, "It wants a drink." The Beast, It, or whatever you decide to call this addictive voice is the animal part of you, the instinctual part of your brain that only wants you to use. It is dumb; its only answer to any problem is drinking, drug use, or another addictive behavior. It might say something like, "Hey, you haven't played video games for a month. It would feel so good to just play one round of Black Ops." Your addictive voice doesn't care about anything else, including how relapsing may hurt you.

BEWARE OF EUPHORIC RECALL

Many people who have had problems with addiction find themselves thinking about the fun times they had when they were using or engaging in addictive behaviors. This is called euphoric recall. It can bring a smile to your face when you think about or talk about those times. However, letting yourself think this way is risky, because thinking about and talking about the "good times" you had can trigger cravings. You might find yourself thinking, "Would it really be so bad if I just did it one more time?" Of course, it's rarely just one time. Try to get yourself to recall the bad times you had as a result of your addiction any time you start thinking about using again. And be realistic about how much the bad aspects outnumber the good. Do this each and every time you think about the fun of using.

It's the primitive part of your brain—the part that seeks pleasure and avoids pain—that is in control of this voice. This primitive brain is sometimes called the reptilian brain because reptiles have the same brain structure as humans, but they don't have the thinking parts in their brains. Learn to recognize this addictive voice and talk back to it. For example, if you are craving alcohol, you can say to yourself, "It wants a drink, but I don't drink." You control whether you listen to your Beast. Some people even think about training their addictions as "putting the Chimp back in its cage." This may sound silly, but give it a try. It works well for many people. If this approach interests you, check out the Rational Recovery website rational.org. You can also learn more about Rational Recovery on page 105.

Finish the Story

One strategy that many find especially helpful is finishing the story. If you catch yourself thinking about how great it would be to start back with your addictive behavior, finish the story by spelling out what would likely happen next, and then next after that, and so on. Here's an example:

> "It would be so great to get high just once with my friends! They're all passing around a blunt and one hit wouldn't hurt, right?" That's how the story starts. Now add the rest: "I could do that and get away with it, maybe once. But then I'd want to do it again, and again. Pretty soon I'll be back to using every day. Then my parents will catch me because they drug test me. Once that happens, they'll take the keys to the car. Then I'll be stuck at home. That will lead to more fights with them, and we've been doing so well together. Why spoil that? Then I'll have to regain their trust, which could take weeks or months. In the meantime, I'll miss out on some fun times with friends over the summer just because I decided to take that first hit. Maybe I'll pass . . ."

Think through any cravings or urges you have by imagining the entire set of consequences that could occur if you give in. For example, if you are thinking of getting high, start by picturing the enjoyment of it. Then imagine how you start coughing, which makes it hard to even walk up the stairs. Picture coming down from the high, yelling at your family, and leaving the house in anger when they threaten you with consequences. Then imagine being arrested for possession, going to court, and being placed on probation or going to jail. When you get to the worst possible thing that could happen, ask yourself if the short-lived high is worth the price you might pay.

Urge Surfing

"I always used to cut myself when I'd get upset at my parents or my boyfriend. It helped at first and took the pain away. I even liked the scars. But after I started cutting deeper and more often, it didn't seem to help as much. Since I'm feeling better about myself since starting therapy, I think of 'riding the wave' when I get those urges. Listening to music, using an aroma diffuser, or even just going for a walk help me now."

• • • •

Another strategy you can try is called urge surfing. Imagine that you are riding a wave in the ocean. It seems overwhelming at first, as if it will drown you. But if you just ride it out and wait for it to break, you'll be fine. The urge to use can feel similarly overwhelming, but if you ride it out, it passes. So if you get a craving or urge to use, wait it out. Do something to distract yourself until the urge passes. You can try one of the healthy substitutes on page 17.

Switching Seats on the *Titanic*

Once you've been sober for a while, it can be tempting to switch to a different drug or type of alcohol. Maybe you had a problem with hard liquor but think you could control your use of beer or wine. Or if you had a problem with marijuana, you might think it would be safe to switch to alcohol instead.

The *Titanic* was the large ocean liner that sank in 1912 after hitting an iceberg in the North Atlantic. So "switching seats on the *Titanic*" means that even when you choose a different drug (like choosing a different seat on the *Titanic*), you'll still go down with the ship. You might be able to use a different drug and not get addicted at first, but the chances are high that you will develop an addiction.

Even worse, using a different mind-altering drug increases the chance that you will relapse on your drug of choice (the one you liked the most). Using other drugs can trigger a craving for your drug of choice. It's as if your brain is thinking, "Hey, this new drug is pretty good. But what I really crave is cocaine–nothing like that high!" The safest approach in recovering from an addiction is always complete abstinence. If you choose to switch to something different anyway, pay close attention to your behavior. Ask your family and friends to pay attention as well, since they may notice problems before you do.

Fact-Check Your Thoughts

Thinking irrationally can make you more likely to relapse. So if you find yourself coming up with reasons to use, hang out with drug-using friends, or put yourself in other risky situations, ask yourself these questions:

- If I use, what is the best thing that could happen?
- What is the worst thing that could happen?
- Knowing myself, what is the most likely thing that will happen?
- What steps can I take to reduce my risk?
- How will I feel if I do relapse? Is this behavior worth the risk?

Your thoughts can trigger relapse when you are having trouble coping with a feeling, a person, or a bad situation. These thoughts might sound like, "I can't deal with this!" "It's too much!" or "I would feel so much better if . . ."

Telling yourself you can't handle something without slipping into addictive behavior is an example of an inaccurate or irrational thought. Of course you can handle situations without drugs or alcohol! You've done it many times before. It may be harder to handle now, or more unpleasant. It may feel like you can't handle it. But feelings aren't facts. You *can* handle it.

Mindfulness

The practice of mindfulness has been around for thousands of years. It's a way of being more present in your day-to-day life. Mindfulness is also an important part of DBT (see page 117). Since addiction is often about escaping from the present, learning ways to deal with the present moment can help reduce your desire to engage in addictive behavior. Mindfulness can help you stop overfocusing on worries about what might happen in the future, as well as avoid dwelling on unpleasant things that have happened in the past.

One of the easiest ways to practice mindfulness is to focus on your breath. Breathing in to the count of five and out to the count of five while turning all your attention to your breathing can help you relax as well as reduce your anxiety. It can help to think of your airway as a vase: the opening is your mouth and the foot is in the pit of your stomach. While you breathe in, imagine you are filling the vase with your breath from the bottom all the way up to the top. As you breathe out, imagine emptying the vase the opposite way, starting at the top. You can't control a lot of what happens around you, but you can control your breath. Try practicing this intentional breathing daily, since the more you practice, the quicker your body will respond when you need it.

Another mindfulness technique is reminding yourself that your thoughts and feelings aren't facts. Thinking that you'll never be able to beat addiction is an example of negative self-talk. You may have worries like this, but try flipping these thoughts to be more positive. Telling yourself that you can do it and that you won't give up is an example of positive self-talk. Remember that when negative thoughts and feelings pop up, you can notice them and then try to let them go. It can help to imagine them fading away slowly or blowing away in the breeze.

Noticing the things around you is another way to practice mindfulness. For example, if you're outside, pay close attention to what you see. Notice the trees, flowers, and clouds; notice the feel of the breeze, the warmth of the sun, and the sounds of birds or other animals. Feel the texture of a leaf, a blade of grass, or the petals of a flower. Some people stand barefoot on the ground and feel a connection or energy boost from Earth's magnetism. This is called grounding.

Mindfulness techniques can help you stay grounded and appreciate the present moment. By avoiding dwelling on the past or worrying about the future, your ability to avoid relapse will grow.

> ## ⚡ TIP!
>
> ### Savoring Your Experiences
>
> Savoring means taking the time to really enjoy something. For example, you might savor something you like to eat or drink, such as a big piece of chocolate cake or a perfectly ripe and juicy apple. But savoring is also a useful coping strategy. When you're having a positive experience, such as a good conversation with friends or family or a nice walk outdoors feeling the sunlight on your face, without engaging in your addictive behaviors, take a few moments to let those good feelings sink in. This helps good feelings stick with you.

Assertiveness

Being able to stand up for yourself and not give in to peer pressure is an important skill to have in recovery. Not only do you need to learn to say no to the temptation to use, you also need to be able to speak up and ask for what you need at home, at school, with friends, and in romantic relationships. Holding onto anger and resentment is a definite relapse trigger.

Being assertive is the middle ground between being passive (not ever speaking up for yourself) and aggressive (screaming and yelling to get what you want). Assertiveness is telling others how you feel and what you would like or need while still respecting their feelings and point of view.

Here's an example. If your friends invite you to a party where you know they'll be using drugs, you have a choice as to how you respond. A passive response might be, "Oh, I don't know. Maybe I'll come if I'm not busy. We'll see . . ." An aggressive response might be, "You know I'm trying to quit! How dare you ask me!" An assertive response would be, "Thanks, but I've been sober for a month and I don't want to take a chance of relapsing. Have fun!"

For more advice on assertiveness, check out the "Assertiveness" page at teenshealth.org.

Flashcards

Keeping flashcards with you for times when you are tempted is another useful technique. Write some of your reasons not to fall back into addictive behavior or things you can do to avoid it. Examples could include:

- I like the freedom I have and don't want to give it up.
- My little brother or sister looks up to me. I don't want to let them down.
- Leave this party NOW! If I wait too long, I know what will happen.
- Why ruin all my hard work for one night of partying?
- I have a lot to live for.
- Things are going great. Why spoil it?

You can carry your flashcards with you or take pictures of them and keep them on your phone. Or write your reasons in a note-taking app so you can add to your list whenever you think of new ones. You can also include pictures of people you love and don't want to let down. You might keep pictures of them in your wallet or set their picture as the wallpaper on your phone, tablet, or computer so you see it often.

Recordings

Try having people you care about and trust record short audio or video clips that you can carry with you. Have these trusted people say something about how they care about you and give reasons for you not to fall back into addictive behavior. Sometimes just seeing the people you care about or hearing their voices can break through your denial enough to pull you back from the edge of the cliff.

Keep in mind that you can use as many or as few of these coping strategies as you would like. It may take you time to figure out which ones work best for you. Think of them as tools in your recovery toolbox.

Honesty Is the Best Policy

When trying to overcome an addiction and avoid relapse, honesty is key. Addictions depend on lies to keep going: lies to your parents, lies to your teachers, lies to your significant other, and even lies to yourself. Each lie you tell makes it easier to tell more lies—about where you are, who you're with, what you're doing, and why you're acting the way that you are. Honesty is like an antidote. Promising yourself that you won't lie anymore makes it easier not to use because if you do use, you'll end up lying to someone about it. It's easier to stick with the truth—you won't have to make up excuses and then remember which lies you told.

Drug Testing

Drug testing is a part of the treatment plan at most addiction treatment centers. It provides additional motivation for you not to go back to using drugs. Knowing you are going to be tested and that there will be consequences if you test positive can help when you are feeling tempted to use drugs again. Also, it gives you a great excuse you can use with friends. If someone offers you a blunt, you can say, "Sorry, I'm being drug tested. I can't take the chance."

Drug-testing kits are available in stores and online. Your doctor can also prescribe drug tests. You might go to a lab where they will take a urine sample. Some programs require that someone watch you while you give your sample to be sure you don't try to alter the results. This can be embarrassing, but worth it if it keeps you on track. If you are on probation or in a drug treatment program, resist the urge to attempt to beat a drug test or alter the results. If you are caught, chances are you'll have to stay on probation or in your program for a longer period of time.

Handling a Slip or Relapse

So you've tried all these strategies and you still slipped or relapsed. While it may feel like the end of the world and a complete failure, that's usually not true. Sure, it feels bad to slip or relapse. But it's also an opportunity to improve your recovery plan. You'll need to do some investigation to figure out how it happened and what you could have done differently to prevent it. As bad as slips or relapses may feel, learning from them can help improve your chances of avoiding them in the future

After a slip or relapse, ask yourself these questions:

- When did you first start thinking of using again?
- What thoughts were going through your head?
- What feelings were you having at the time?
- What kept you from slipping earlier?
- Who were you with when it happened, and how was that related to your slip or relapse?

- What can you do differently to help yourself stay strong and avoid slipping or relapsing the next time?

By answering these questions, you can figure out what to do the next time you feel like using.

Taking It Day by Day

Recovering from addictions is a difficult journey for many. And most who take on the challenge will relapse along the way. It might seem at times like getting over your addiction is an overwhelming task and like you'll never get better. It's true that recovering from an addiction takes a lot of effort, not just in learning about addictions and why they are hard to quit or control, but in avoiding the many temptations to go back to old behaviors, even when you know they've caused you problems. At the same time, relapse prevention is all about gaining valuable life skills that will help you deal with your feelings, overcome boredom, and develop healthier relationships.

Recovery can often feel like you're walking up a down escalator. If you stop moving, you'll slide back. But if you keep walking, and if you get up when you fall, your legs will get stronger and it will get easier to manage as time goes on. As they say in 12-step programs, "Take it one day at a time," and "Keep coming back—it works if you work it!"

A Concluding Note

I hope that by reading this book, you've learned a lot about addictions, the ways they can interfere with your life, and the strategies you can use to help you avoid them or overcome them if you have them.

If you are worried about your use and need help, I encourage you to reach out to a friend or an adult you trust who can help you find treatment or a program that works for you. It's not easy to admit that you need help, but the potential consequences of addictions are too great to deal with all on your own. For more information on addictions and support groups, check out the resources on page 145. If you want to contact me, you can send me an email at help4kids@freespirit.com.

—Dr. James J. Crist

Glossary of Terms About Addiction

Acid: Another name for LSD.

Addict: Someone who is addicted to a drug and is unable to stop using it, even after the drug use causes problems. An addict is someone with a substance use disorder. People who are addicted to drugs sometimes call themselves addicts as a reminder than they cannot use drugs anymore without it causing serious problems. (Sometimes people who have compulsive, harmful behaviors such as gambling may also be described as addicts).

Addiction: A brain disease that makes it hard for people who use drugs or alcohol, or engage in other addictive behaviors, to stop or control their use, even when it is causing problems for them or others.

Alateen: A self-help organization for teens who have parents or other family members who are addicted to alcohol or drugs. Alateen meetings help teens deal with their feelings and share ideas on how to handle the problem.

Alcohol: A chemical (ethanol) that is present in wine, beer, and hard liquor, among other beverages. Alcohol is a depressant drug and changes the way people feel and act.

Alcoholic: Someone who continues to drink alcohol even when it causes problems for them or their families. An alcoholic is someone with an alcohol use disorder. People who are addicted to alcohol will sometimes refer to themselves as alcoholics as a reminder that they cannot drink alcohol without it causing problems.

Alcoholics Anonymous (AA): A self-help organization for people who want to stop drinking alcohol. At AA meetings, alcoholics can get help and support for staying away from alcohol.

135

Amotivational syndrome: This can occur for some marijuana users after using the drug repeatedly. They no longer feel motivated to do much of anything, such as completing homework or helping around the house.

Amphetamine: A stimulant drug that can give the user more energy, focus, and confidence. In higher doses, it can create a sense of euphoria. It can also make the user more depressed (especially when they stop taking it) or see or hear things that aren't really there (hallucinations).

Bad trip: This occurs when someone has a bad experience while getting high on LSD or other hallucinogenic drugs such as peyote or mushrooms. Bad trips can be very scary because the person does not know if what is happening is real or not.

Bath salts: These contain a manufactured form of the drug cathinone, which is a stimulant. Bath salts are often sold as other products to disguise the fact that they are actually illegal drugs.

Blackout: This happens when someone drinks so much alcohol that they cannot remember what happened when they were drinking. This is dangerous because they might hurt themselves or others without remembering it.

Binge: Using a lot of alcohol or drugs or engaging in other addictive behavior such as overeating or gaming for a long period of time, much more than usual. Drinking alcohol all weekend or eating large amounts of food to the point of feeling sick are examples of this.

Blood alcohol concentration (BAC): The amount of alcohol present in the bloodstream. Also called blood alcohol level. It is used to determine whether someone can be arrested for driving while intoxicated (DWI or DUI). For teens and adults under 21, *any* amount of alcohol in the system is considered breaking the law.

Blunt: A cigar wrapper that is filled with marijuana.

Bong: A device people use to smoke marijuana that filters the smoke through water.

CBD oil: Cannabidiol (CBD) oil is a legal (in many, but not all, states) marijuana extract that is being sold as a drug that may relieve pain, anxiety, and improve sleep without getting the user high.

Clean: People may describe themselves as clean when they have stopped using drugs and are trying to keep from going back to using them again. Similarly, people use the word *sober* when they are not drinking alcohol anymore.

Cocaine: A stimulant drug made from the leaves of the coca plant. It can give the user more energy, focus, and feelings of euphoria. In larger amounts, it can make them more irritable or paranoid.

Cognitive behavioral therapy (CBT): A treatment strategy that focuses on changing how people think about things to help them feel better and make better decisions.

Counseling: Also called therapy, counseling involves meeting and talking with a counselor (or therapist) to get help or advice about problems, such as being addicted to alcohol, drugs, or other activities. Counseling can help people learn to handle problems with their behavior or their feelings.

Crack: A very addictive form of cocaine that is smoked. It gives an intense high but can be even more dangerous than powdered cocaine.

Cravings: Feelings of wanting to use alcohol or drugs or engage in addictive behavior. Cravings make it harder to stop using and avoid going back to using or engaging in other addictive behavior.

Crystal methamphetamine: Also called crystal meth or Ice, this is a stimulant drug that gives the user more energy and improves their mood.

Denial: Someone in denial tells themselves that their problem with addiction isn't that bad and that others are overreacting. Denial keeps people from feeling bad about their behavior and allows addictive behavior to continue.

Depressant: A type of drug that can calm the nervous system, causing relaxation or sleep. Examples include alcohol; benzodiazepines including Valium, Xanax, and Klonopin; and GHB.

Dialectical behavior therapy (DBT): A treatment strategy that helps people manage their emotions and relationships in healthier ways.

Dopamine: A brain chemical, known as a neurotransmitter, that makes activities more enjoyable and makes you want to do more of those activities. Most addictive behaviors increase levels of dopamine in the brain.

Drug: A chemical that changes how nerve cells (called neurons) communicate with each other. People use drugs to change their feelings and their behavior. Examples include marijuana, cocaine, heroin, OxyContin, nicotine, and LSD. Alcohol contains the drug ethanol.

Drunk: When someone has had so much alcohol that their actions are affected. Some drunk behaviors include acting silly, not being able to walk straight, getting sleepy, being loud, or becoming angry for no reason. People act in different ways when they are drunk. Driving when drunk is illegal and extremely dangerous.

DXM (cough syrup): This is the active ingredient in some types of cough syrup. People drink large amounts of cough syrup to get high, similar to the high from using PCP. This is sometimes called robotripping.

E-cigarettes: This is a type of cigarette that uses a battery-operated device to vaporize tobacco so the user can breathe it into their lungs. It uses liquid pods that are placed into the device, which are often flavored. These can be used to vaporize tobacco, which contains nicotine, or marijuana, which contains THC.

Ecstasy: A stimulant drug (with hallucinogenic properties), also known as MDMA, Molly, or E, that produces feelings of increased energy, pleasure, emotional closeness with others, and alters the senses, including the sense of time. Ecstasy is popular in clubs and all-night dance parties.

Fentanyl: An opioid-like drug manufactured in a lab that is much stronger than natural opioids such as morphine or heroin. It is much easier to overdose on and is very dangerous. Drug dealers sometimes add fentanyl to heroin to make it cheaper for them to sell.

Flashback: When someone starts hallucinating again after not using LSD or other hallucinogenic drugs for a while. A flashback can happen years after someone stops using LSD. Flashbacks are often upsetting.

GHB (gamma hydroxybutyrate): This is a depressant drug that may be used by bodybuilders as a supplement to build muscle or reduce fat. It is also a type of date-rape drug because it can be added to a drink to sedate someone to the point that they cannot react if someone tries to have sex with them.

Hallucinogen: A type of drug that distorts the way the user sees objects or events, or makes them see or hear things that aren't really there. Examples include LSD, certain mushrooms, ketamine, ecstasy, and marijuana at higher doses.

Hangover: A sick feeling the morning after drinking a lot of alcohol. People with a hangover usually feel tired and have a bad headache.

Heroin: A highly addictive narcotic drug. It makes people relaxed or sleepy and can relieve pain. Overdoses frequently lead to death.

Inhalant: A chemical that is sniffed or inhaled through the nose or mouth in order to get high. Examples include sniffing glue, paint thinners, and gasoline.

Ketamine: This is a hallucinogenic drug that can cause dream-like states and a feeling of floating or being separated from the body. It can also be used as a date-rape drug because it can make people unable to respond or fight back if assaulted sexually and may prevent them from even remembering it. More recently it is being used to treat depression when administered by medical professionals.

LSD: A hallucinogenic drug, also called acid, that makes people see and hear things that are not really there. LSD changes your sense of time, place, and reality.

Marijuana (cannabis): A hallucinogenic drug, also called grass, dope, and weed, among other names, that contains the chemical THC. Possible effects include feeling relaxed or high, feeling less anxious, and making it easier to sleep. Some people get anxious or paranoid and hallucinate when using marijuana, especially at higher doses.

Moderation Management (MM): A self-help organization designed to help people with an alcohol addiction take control over their behavior, whether they choose to abstain completely from alcohol or try to control their use by setting safer limits.

Mushrooms: These are a type of mushroom, also called shrooms or magic mushrooms, that cause people to hallucinate when eaten.

Narcotic: Also called opioids, this type of drug relieves pain or helps people sleep. Examples include morphine, heroin, Vicodin, and OxyContin. Higher doses can create a feeling of euphoria or being high.

Narcotics Anonymous (NA): A self-help organization for people who want to stop using drugs. People who are addicted to drugs go to NA meetings to get help and support for staying away from drugs.

Neurotransmitter: A brain chemical that alters how nerve cells communicate with each other, causing changes in emotions, thoughts, and actions.

Nicotine: This drug is the active chemical found in tobacco. Nicotine helps people calm down, reduces appetite, and can make it easier to focus.

Overdose: When someone takes too much of a drug to the point that it makes them pass out or die by stopping their heart or breathing.

PCP (phencyclidine): Sometimes called Angel Dust, this is a hallucinogenic drug that comes in a white powder that can be sniffed or dissolved in water or in a liquid form can be sprayed onto leafy material such as oregano and smoked. It typically causes hallucinations and a sense of being separated from the body.

Peyote: This is a small cactus that contains the chemical mescaline. Parts of it are cut from the plant (called buttons) and dried. The dried buttons are eaten or soaked in water. It causes hallucinations.

Rational Recovery: A self-help group for people with alcohol or drug problems who are trying to help themselves drink or use less or stop completely. It is similar AA or NA, but people in RR use different ways to stop using alcohol or drugs.

Recovery: Someone is "in recovery" or "recovering" when they have stopped using alcohol or other drugs, or have stopped engaging in other addictive behaviors, and are working hard at not using them again because their use was causing problems. People say they are "recovering" instead of "recovered" because if they go back to using, the same problems will likely come back.

Rehab (residential treatment center): A place where people can go to get help with drinking, drug use, or other addictive behaviors when they can't stop on their own or with counseling. People will stay in rehab a month or longer depending on how bad their problem is.

Relapse: This is when someone starts to drink, use drugs, or engage in other addictive behavior again after stopping for a period of time. Relapse is common when people are just starting treatment, though it can happen anytime to anyone. Learning how to avoid relapse is part of the recovery process.

Rohypnol (flunitrazepam): This is a depressant drug, commonly called roofies, and can be used to put people to sleep prior to surgery. Rohypnol is also known as a date-rape drug.

Robotripping: Drinking large amounts of cough syrup that contains DXM to get high.

Roid rage: When someone who is using steroids gets very angry and they have trouble controlling their behavior.

Self-injury: Hurting oneself on purpose by scratching, cutting, or burning in order to make bad feelings such as anger, sadness, or numbness go away.

Sexting: Sending or receiving sexual messages, pictures, or videos. It is illegal for teens to send pictures of themselves or others because it is seen as child pornography, which carries serious legal consequences.

Shooting up: Using a needle or syringe to take a shot of a drug, usually heroin or cocaine.

SMART Recovery: A self-help organization that is an alternative to AA or NA. In SMART Recovery, people learn to think about addiction differently and use cognitive-behavioral strategies to help themselves quit drugs, alcohol, or other activities.

Sober: When a person who is addicted to alcohol is no longer using it and is actively trying to not go back to drinking.

Sobriety: People say that they are "in sobriety" when they are not using alcohol or drugs anymore.

Steroids: Also known as Juice or roids, these are chemicals that normally are used to treat certain medical conditions, such as asthma. Bodybuilders may use them to make their muscles bigger and stronger. Some people get very angry when using steroids.

Stimulant: A drug that speeds up the body, increases energy, helps with focus, produces feelings of euphoria, and keeps the user from sleeping. Examples include cocaine, crack, crystal meth, and ecstasy. Adderall and Ritalin are also stimulant drugs, but they are legal to use when prescribed for mental health disorders such as ADHD. They can also be abused in higher doses.

Synthetic marijuana: Sold at gas stations or other convenience stores, it is often called Spice or K2. It is made of herbs and spices that are sprayed with dangerous chemicals and when smoked gives people a similar high to marijuana.

Tolerance: This occurs when using drugs or alcohol (or engaging in other addictive behaviors) no longer feels as enjoyable as it once was. This triggers people to use more drugs or alcohol (or spend more time on addictive behaviors) so they can get the same rewarding feeling.

Treatment: People who are in treatment are going to a counseling program to get help with their drug or alcohol use. Treatment can also help people deal with feelings or behavior problems.

Vaping: This refers to using an e-cigarette device to vaporize a liquid containing nicotine or THC to breathe it into the lungs. It uses pods that are placed into the device, which are often flavored.

Withdrawal: This happens when someone stops using drugs or alcohol after having been physically addicted. Their body has trouble adjusting and this causes symptoms that can include irritability, anxiety, sleep disturbance, anger, and physical pain, depending on the substance used.

Books

Beautiful Boy: A Father's Journey Through His Son's Addiction by David Sheff (New York: Houghton Mifflin Harcourt, 2008). This book describes a father's experiences dealing with his son Nic's addiction. It was made into a movie in 2018.

Clean: Overcoming Addiction and Ending America's Greatest Tragedy by David Sheff (New York: Houghton Mifflin Harcourt, 2013). This book explores how addiction is treated and why many do not benefit from traditional treatment. The author reviews how addiction develops and what treatment strategies work.

Don't Let Emotions Run Your Life for Teens by Sheri Van Dijk (Oakland, CA: Instant Help Books, 2011). A workbook based in dialectical behavior therapy to help you learn to manage and cope with emotions.

Tweak: Growing Up on Methamphetamines by Nic Sheff (New York: Atheneum Books for Young Readers, 2008). This book was written by a young adult who started using alcohol and drugs as a teenager. It describes his experiences and the path he took toward recovery. Nic Sheff wrote this book after his father wrote the book *Beautiful Boy*.

We All Fall Down: Living with Addiction by Nic Sheff (New York: Little, Brown Books for Young Readers, 2011). This sequel to his earlier book, *Tweak*, describes the author's relapses and experiences in rehab centers after initially stopping his use.

What Are My Rights? Q&A About Teens and the Law by Thomas Jacobs, J.D. (Minneapolis: Free Spirit Publishing, 2018). This book provides answers to your questions about legal rights for young people, exploring more than 100 legal questions pertaining specifically to teens.

Self-Help and Other Organizations

Al-Anon/Alateen
al-anon.org • (757) 563-1600 • wso@al-anon.org
Meeting information: 1-888-425-2666

Alcoholics Anonymous
aa.org • (212) 870-3400

Cocaine Anonymous
ca.org • (310) 559-5833 • cawso@ca.org

Crystal Meth Anonymous
crystalmeth.org • 1-855-METH-FREE / 1-855-638-4373

Families Anonymous
familiesanonymous.org • 1-800-736-9805 • info@familiesanonymous.org

Food Addicts Anonymous
foodaddictsanonymous.org • (772) 878-9657

Food Addicts in Recovery Anonymous
foodaddicts.org • (781) 932-6300 • fa@foodaddicts.org

Gamblers Anonymous
gamblersanonymous.org • (626) 960-3500
isomain@gamblersanonymous.org

Heroin Anonymous
heroinanonymous.org

Marijuana Anonymous
marijuana-anonymous.org • 1-800-766-6779

Moderation Management
moderation.org • mm@moderation.org

Narcotics Anonymous
na.org • (818) 773-9999

Nar-Anon Family Groups (for family and friends of addicted persons)
nar-anon.org • 1-800-477-6291
wso@nar-anon.org (English) • osm@nar-anon.org (Español)

National Association for Children of Addiction
nacoa.net • 1-888-55-4COAS / 1-888-554-2627 • nacoa@nacoa.org

National Council on Problem Gambling
ncpgambling.org • (202) 547-9204 • ncpg@ncpgambling.org

National Institute on Alcohol Abuse and Alcoholism (NIAAA)
niaaa.nih.gov • (301) 443-3860 • niaaaweb-r@exchange.nih.gov

National Institute on Drug Abuse
drugabuse.gov • (301) 443-1124

Nicotine Anonymous
nicotine-anonymous.org • 1-877-TRY-NICA / 1-877-879-6422

Overeaters Anonymous
oa.org • (505) 891-2664

Rational Recovery Systems
rational.org • (530) 621-2667

ReStart (Internet and Gaming Addiction Recovery)
netaddictionrecovery.com • hello@restartlife.com

Secular Organizations for Sobriety
sosobriety.org • (323) 666-4295

SMART (Self-Management and Recovery Training)
smartrecovery.org • (440) 951-5357

Sexaholics Anonymous (SA)
sa.org • (615) 370-6062

Sex and Love Addicts Anonymous (SLAA)
slaafws.org • (210) 828-7900

Women for Sobriety
womenforsobriety.org • (215) 536-8026

Websites

Above the Influence • abovetheinfluence.com
This site is designed to help you stand up to negative pressures. It provides the latest facts on addiction to help you be more aware of the influences around you so you can make your own decisions.

Game Quitters • gamequitters.com
This site provides information on gaming and ways to get it under control. You can take a quiz to see if your use is addictive. Other resources include how to find support groups. A section for adults is also provided.

NIDA for Teens • teens.drugabuse.gov
This site provides accurate scientific information on how alcohol and drugs affect the body and brain. You can take quizzes and participate in research as well. A Spanish version of the site is available.

Tech Addiction • techaddiction.ca
This is a treatment center and information service for people struggling to control their use of technology. It includes in-person therapy, downloadable self-help guides, practical advice, unbiased research, and useful information to anyone who believes that their excessive use of tech is interfering with the quality of their life.

Bibliography

American Academy of Neurology. "Drinking Heavy Amounts of Alcohol Shrinks Your Brain." ScienceDaily. May 3, 2007. sciencedaily.com/releases /2007/05/070502172317.htm.

American Lung Association. "What's in a Cigarette?" Updated May 27, 2020. lung.org/quit-smoking/smoking-facts/whats-in-a-cigarette.

Ashwood Staff. "The Real Story About Video Game Addiction." Ashwood Recovery. July 29, 2015. ashwoodrecovery.com/blog/video -game-addiction.

Baylor College of Medicine. "Activating Dopamine Neurons Could Turn Off Binge-Like Eating Behavior." ScienceDaily. August 8, 2016. sciencedaily.com/releases/2016/08/160808115604.htm.

Beck, Aaron T., Fred D. Wright, Cory F. Newman, and Bruce S. Liese. *Cognitive Therapy of Substance Abuse*. New York: The Guilford Press, 2013.

Bipolar Network News. "Alcohol Use Disorders That Begin Before Age 21 May Cause Lasting Changes to Amygdala." *Bipolar Network News* 23, no. 3 (October 2019): 5.

Bradford, Alina. "Ayahuasca: Psychedelic Tea from the Amazon." Live Science. May 20, 2016. livescience.com/54813-ayahuasca.html.

Brawley, Otis. "How Quickly Does Lung Cancer Develop for Smokers?" *The Chart* (blog). April 20, 2011. thechart.blogs.cnn.com/2011/04/20 /how-quickly-does-lung-cancer-develop-for-smokers.

Burgess, Lana. "What Is Hallucinogen-Persisting Perception Disorder?" Medical News Today. March 16, 2018. medicalnewstoday.com/articles /320181.

CDC. "Electronic Cigarettes." Office on Smoking and Health. Updated February 25, 2020. cdc.gov/tobacco/basic_information/e-cigarettes /index.htm.

Chicago Tribune. "Mobile Phones Linked to Anxiety and Severe Depression in Teens." *Young Post*. December 31, 2017. scmp.com/yp /discover/lifestyle/features/article/3068739/mobile-phones-linked -anxiety-and-severe-depression.

Conrad, Brent. "Study: 85% of Teens Play Video Games—1 in 10 Have Problematic Use." TechAddiction.ca. 2013. techaddiction.ca/most-teens -play-video-games.html.

———. "Video Game Addiction Statistics—Facts, Figures, Percentages, and Numbers." TechAddiction.ca. Accessed April 9, 2020. techaddiction.ca/video_game_addiction_statistics.html.

Conterio, Karen, and Wendy Lader. *Bodily Harm: The Breakthrough Healing Program for Self-Injurers.* New York: Hyperion, 1998.

DeAngelis, Tori. "Who Self-Injures?" *Monitor on Psychology* 46, no. 7 (July/August 2015): 60.

Drug Policy Alliance. "Race and the Drug War." Accessed April 9, 2020. drugpolicy.org/issues/race-and-drug-war.

Dryden-Edwards, Roxanne. "Alcohol and Teens." MedicineNet. Accessed April 9, 2020. medicinenet.com/alcohol_and_teens /article.htm#alcohol_and_teens_facts.

Fadiman, James. *The Psychedelic Explorer's Guide.* Rochester, VT: Park Street Press, 2011.

Fanning, Patrick, and John T. O'Neill. *The Addiction Workbook: A Step-by- Step Guide to Quitting Alcohol and Drugs.* Oakland, CA: New Harbinger Publications, 1996.

FBI: UCR. "2016 Crime in the United States." US Department of Justice. 2017. ucr.fbi.gov/crime-in-the-u.s/2016/crime-in-the-u.s.-2016 /topic-pages/tables/table-20.

Federal Student Aid. "Students with Criminal Convictions Have Limited Eligibility for Federal Student Aid." US Department of Education. Accessed April 9, 2020. studentaid.gov/understand-aid/eligibility /requirements/criminal-convictions.

Gold, Mark S. "Stages of Change." *Psych Central.* Updated April 11, 2020. psychcentral.com/lib/stages-of-change/?all=1%20and%20 verywellmind.com/the-stages-of-change-model-of-overcoming -addiction-21961.

Grandclerc, Salome, Diane De Labrouhe, Michel Spodenkiewicz, Jonathan Lachal, and Marie-Rose Moro. "Relations Between Nonsuicidal Self-Injury and Suicidal Behavior in Adolescence: A Systematic Review." *PLoS One* 11, no. 4 (2016): e0153760. doi: 10.1371/journal.pone.0153760.

Greenblatt, James M. "Biology of the Binge: Food, Mood, and Serotonin." *Psychology Today*. April 18, 2014. psychologytoday.com/us/blog/the -breakthrough-depression-solution/201404/biology-the-binge-food -mood-and-serotonin.

Griffin-Shelley, Eric. *Adolescent Sex and Love Addicts*. Westport, CT: Praeger Publishers, 1994.

HAMS. "How Alcohol Is Metabolized in the Human Body." Accessed April 10, 2020. hams.cc/metabolism.

"High School Gambling Fact Sheet." National Council on Problem Gambling. ncpgambling.org/files/HS_Fact_Sheet.pdf.

Hoeg, Natalie. "Microdosing LSD." AddictionCenter.com. Updated April 29, 2020. addictioncenter.com/drugs/hallucinogens/lsd-addiction /microdosing-lsd.

Hoyle, Gideon. "What Is a Wet Drug?" Promises Austin. December 24, 2016. promises.com/addiction-blog/what-is-a-wet-drug.

Jiang, Jingjing. "How Teens and Parents Navigate Screen Time and Device Distractions." Pew Research Center. August 22, 2018. pewresearch.org/internet/2018/08/22/how-teens-and-parents-navigate -screen-time-and-device-distractions.

Jones, Maggie. "What Teenagers Are Learning from Online Porn." *New York Times Magazine*. February 7, 2018. nytimes.com/2018/02/07 /magazine/teenagers-learning-online-porn-literacy-sex-education.html.

Kann, Laura, Tim McManus, William A. Harris, Shari L. Shanklin, Katherine H. Flint, Barbara Queen, Richard Lowry, et al. *Youth Risk Behavior Surveillance—United States, 2017*. MMWR Surveillance Summary 67, no. 8. Centers for Disease Control and Prevention, 2018.

Knutson, Ted. "Video Games Can Be a Gateway to Problem Gambling, FTC Warned." *Forbes*. August 8, 2019. forbes.com/sites/tedknutson /2019/08/08/video-games-can-be-a-gateway-to-problem-gambling-ftc -warned/#26e9227d978a.

Krans, Brian. "Why Researchers Say You Might Want to Smoke Marijuana Rather Than Vape It." Healthline. December 10, 2018. healthline.com/health-news/why-vaping-marijuana-gets-you-a-lot -higher-than-smoking-it.

Lemmens, Jeroen S., Patti M. Valkenburg, and Jochen Peter. "The Effects of Pathological Gaming on Aggressive Behavior." *Journal of Youth and Adolescence* 40, no. 1 (January 2011): 38–47. doi: 10.1007/s10964-010-9558-x.

Lyons, Libby. "Understanding the Differences Between Food Addictions and an Eating Disorder." EatingDisorderHope.com. Reviewed March 18, 2017. eatingdisorderhope.com/blog/food-addictions-eating-disorder.

Margolies, Lynn. "Teens and Internet Pornography."PsychCentral. October 8, 2018. psychcentral.com/lib/teens-and-internet-pornography.

Maryland Medical Cannabis Commission. "Process to Legally Obtain Medical Cannabis." Accessed April 10, 2020. mmcc.maryland.gov/Pages/process_to_obtain.aspx.

Milkman, Harvey B., and Stanley G. Sunderwirth. *Craving for Ecstasy: The Consciousness and Chemistry of Escape.* Lexington, MA: Lexington Books, 1987.

Monti, Peter M., Ronald M. Kadden, Damaris J. Rohsenow, Ned L. Cooney, and David B. Abrams. *Treating Alcohol Dependence: A Coping Skills Training Guide.* New York: The Guilford Press, 2002.

Moran, P., C. Coffey, H. Romaniuk, L. Degenhardt, R. Borschmann, and G. C. Patton. "Substance Use in Adulthood Following Adolescent Self-Harm. A Population-Based Cohort Study." *Acta Psychiatrica Scandinavica* 131, no. 1 (January 2015): 61–68. doi: 10.1111/acps.12306.

Murse, Tom. "States Where Smoking Recreational Marijuana Is Legal." ThoughtCo. Updated February 4, 2020. thoughtco.com/states-that-legalized-marijuana-3368391.

National Center for Injury Prevention and Control. "Teen Drivers: Get the Facts." Centers for Disease Control and Prevention. Last reviewed October 30, 2019. cdc.gov/motorvehiclesafety/teen_drivers/teendrivers_factsheet.html.

National Center on Sexual Exploitation. *Pornography and Public Health Research Summary.* NCSE, 2017. endsexualexploitation.org/wp-content/uploads/NCOSE_Pornography-PublicHealth_ResearchSummary_8-2_17_FINAL-with-logo.pdf.

NEDA. "Statistics & Research on Eating Disorders." NEDA. Accessed April 15, 2020. nationaleatingdisorders.org/statistics-research-eating-disorders.

NIAAA. "Underage Drinking." National Institutes of Health.
Updated January 2020. niaaa.nih.gov/publications/brochures-and-fact
-sheets/underage-drinking.

NIDA. "Drug Facts: High School and Youth Trends." National Institutes
of Health, 2016. drugabuse.gov/sites/default/files/df_high_school
_and_youth_trends_june2016_final.pdf.

———. "Drugs, Brains, and Behavior: The Science of Addiction."
NIH Pub. No. 10-5605. National Institutes of Health, 2018.
drugabuse.gov/publications/drugs-brains-behavior-science-addiction
/drug-misuse-addiction.

———. "Marijuana." National Institutes of Health. Updated April 2020.
drugabuse.gov/publications/research-reports/marijuana/marijuana
-addictive.

———. "Synthetic Cannabinoids (K2/Spice)." National Institutes of
Health. Updated April 2016. drugabuse.gov/drugs-abuse/synthetic
-cannabinoids-k2spice.

NIDA for Teens. "Drug Overdoses in Youth." National Institutes of
Health. Updated March 28, 2020. teens.drugabuse.gov/drug-facts
/drug-overdoses-youth.

Pace, Steven. "Action Video Games Improve Goal-Directed Reaction
Times, Study Finds." PsyPost. June 23, 2016. psypost.org/2016/06
/action-video-games-improve-goal-directed-reaction-times-study
-finds-43507.

Partnership for Drug-Free Kids. drugfree.org.

PsychGuides.com. "Video Game Addiction Symptoms, Causes, and
Effects." American Addiction Centers. Accessed April 14, 2020.
psychguides.com/behavioral-disorders/video-game-addiction.

Rideout, Victoria, and Michael B. Robb. *The Common Sense Census: Media
Use by Tweens and Teens, 2019*. San Francisco: Common Sense Media,
2019. commonsensemedia.org/sites/default/files/uploads/research
/2019-census-8-to-18-full-report-updated.pdf.

Selby, Emily. "What to Avoid with Psychiatric Medications."
National Alliance on Mental Illness. Updated January 16, 2019.
nami.org/Learn-More/Treatment/Mental-Health-Medications
/What-to-Avoid-with-Psychiatric-Medications.

Shmerling, Robert. "Can Vaping Help You Quit Smoking?" Harvard Health. February 27, 2019. health.harvard.edu/blog/can-vaping-help-you-quit-smoking-2019022716086.

Smith, Cassie, Peter John Herzig, Andrew Davey, Ben Desbrow, and Christopher Irwin. "The Influence of Mixers Containing Artificial Sweetener or Different Doses of Carbohydrate on Breath Alcohol Responses in Females." *Alcoholism* 41, no. 1 (January 2017): 38–45.

Spiegelman, Erica. *Rewired: A Bold New Approach to Addiction and Recovery*. New York: Hatherleigh Press, 2015.

StopBullying.gov. "What Is Cyberbullying?" StopBullying.gov. Last reviewed May 7, 2020. stopbullying.gov/cyberbullying/what-is-it.

Tran, Jessica. "Texting While Driving Laws" Legal Match. Updated June 24, 2018. legalmatch.com/law-library/article/texting-while-driving-laws.html.

Trimpey, Jack. *Rational Recovery: The New Cure for Substance Addiction*. New York: Pocket Books, 1996.

Urschel, Harold C. *Healing the Addicted Brain: The Revolutionary, Science-Based Alcoholism and Addiction Recovery Program*. Naperville, IL: Sourcebooks, 2009.

Watson, Stephanie, and Kristeen Cherney. "The Effects of Sleep Deprivation on Your Body." Healthline. May 15, 2020. healthline.com/health/sleep-deprivation/effects-on-body#1.

WebMD. "Food Addiction." WebMD Medical Reference. Last reviewed August 3, 2018. webmd.com/mental-health/eating-disorders/binge-eating-disorder/mental-health-food-addiction.

Weinstein, Aviv, Abigail Livny, and Abraham Weizman. "New Developments in Brain Research of Internet and Gaming Disorder." *Neuroscience & Biobehavioral Reviews* 75 (April 2017): 314–330.

West, James. "Inside the Chinese Boot Camps Designed to Break Video Game Addiction." *Mother Jones* (March/April 2015). motherjones.com/media/2015/06/chinese-internet-addiction-center-photos.

Index

About the Author

Dr. James J. Crist is a clinical psychologist and certified substance abuse counselor specializing in ADHD, depression, anxiety disorders, bipolar disorder, addictive disorders, relapse prevention, ACOA issues, parenting issues, and anger management. He provides individual and family therapy for children, adolescents, and adults. Dr. Crist also conducts psychological and substance abuse evaluations and gives workshops to community organizations. He resides in the Washington D.C. area. For more information, you can visit his website, jamesjcrist.com. You can also follow him on Facebook (James J. Crist, Ph.D.) and Twitter (@JamesJCristPHD).

• • • • •

Other Great Resources from Free Spirit

The Struggle to Be Strong
True Stories by Teens About Overcoming Tough Times (Updated Edition)
edited by Al Desetta, M.A., and Sybil Wolin, Ph.D.

For ages 13 & up.
184 pp.; PB; 6" x 9".

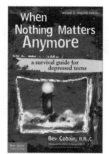

When Nothing Matters Anymore
A Survival Guide for Depressed Teens (Revised & Updated Edition)
by Bev Cobain, R.N.,C.

For ages 13 & up.
176 pp.; PB; 2-color; illust.; 6" x 9".

The Power to Prevent Suicide
A Guide for Teens Helping Teens (Updated Edition)
by Richard E. Nelson, Ph.D., and Judith C. Galas

For ages 11 & up.
128 pp.; PB; 6" x 9".

What Are My Rights?
Q&A About Teens and the Law (Revised & Updated 4th Edition)
by Thomas A. Jacobs, J.D.

For ages 12 & up.
240 pp.; PB; 6" x 9".

Fighting Invisible Tigers
Stress Management for Teens (Revised & Updated 4th Edition)
by Earl Hipp

For ages 11 & up.
144 pp.; PB; 2-color; illust.; 6" x 9".

When a Friend Dies
A Book for Teens About Grieving & Healing (Updated 3rd Edition)
by Marilyn E. Gootman, Ed.D.

For ages 11 & up.
136 pp.; PB; B&W photos; 5" x 7".

Interested in purchasing multiple quantities and receiving volume discounts?
Contact edsales@freespirit.com or call 1.800.735.7323 and ask for Education Sales.

Many Free Spirit authors are available for speaking engagements, workshops, and keynotes.
Contact speakers@freespirit.com or call 1.800.735.7323.

For pricing information, to place an order, or to request a free catalog, contact:

Free Spirit Publishing Inc. • 6325 Sandburg Road, Suite 100 • Minneapolis, MN 55427-3674
toll-free 800.735.7323 • local 612.338.2068 • fax 612.337.5050
help4kids@freespirit.com • freespirit.com